walkermaths 3.8

TIME SERIES

NCEA Level 3 Internal

Second Edition

Charlotte Walker and Victoria Walker

Walker Maths 3.8 Time Series
2nd Edition
Charlotte Walker
Victoria Walker

Designer: Cheryl Smith, Macarn Design
Production controller: Siew Han Ong

Any URLs contained in this publication were checked for currency during the production process. Note, however, that the publisher cannot vouch for the ongoing currency of URLs.

Acknowledgements
Cover photo courtesy of Shutterstock

We wish to thank past and present colleagues who have generously shared their expertise and ideas.

For product information and technology assistance,
in Australia call **1300 790 853**;
in New Zealand call **0800 449 725**

For permission to use material from this text or product, please email **aust.permissions@cengage.com**

National Library of New Zealand Cataloguing-in-Publication Data
A catalogue record for this book is available from the National Library of New Zealand

ISBN 978 0 17 047297 5

Cengage Learning Australia
Level 5, 80 Dorcas Street
Southbank VIC 3006 Australia

Cengage Learning New Zealand
For learning solutions, visit **cengage.co.nz**

Printed in China by 1010 Printing International Limited.
4 5 6 7 26 25

CONTENTS

Glossary

Make your own glossary of key terms:

Term	Definition	Picture/Example
Trend		
Seasonal pattern		
Individual seasonal effect		
Average seasonal effect		
Moving mean		
Centred moving mean		
Residual		
Cyclic pattern		
Recomposition		
Forecast		
Robustness		
Holt-Winters		
Quarter		
Weighted mean		

ISBN: 9780170472975

Introduction

This standard will require you to analyse time series data. More specifically, you will be required to:

- **research** a context in order to **select** an appropriate variable for analysis from an existing data set
- for your investigation identify an appropriate **purpose** that has been developed from research
- select and use appropriate **displays**
- identify **features** in the data including the **trend** and the **seasonal pattern**, and relate these to the **context**
- combine the trend and the seasonal pattern to form a **model**, and discuss its **accuracy**
- use the model to make a **forecast**, and discuss its **accuracy**
- communicate findings in a **conclusion**.

What is time series data?

- This is an ordered sequence of measurements recorded at **regular intervals** over a time period, for example: value of products sold by a shop each day over several months, number of cars passing a particular point per hour, number of heartbeats per minute over an hour, etc.
- Each value is **plotted** as a point on a **line** graph.
- The x-axis is **always** time.
- The variables investigated may be **discrete** or **continuous**.

The purpose of analysing a time series is to use the model to forecast (predict) what will happen in the future.

The statistical enquiry cycle
Your report should connect back to all aspects of the statistical enquiry cycle:

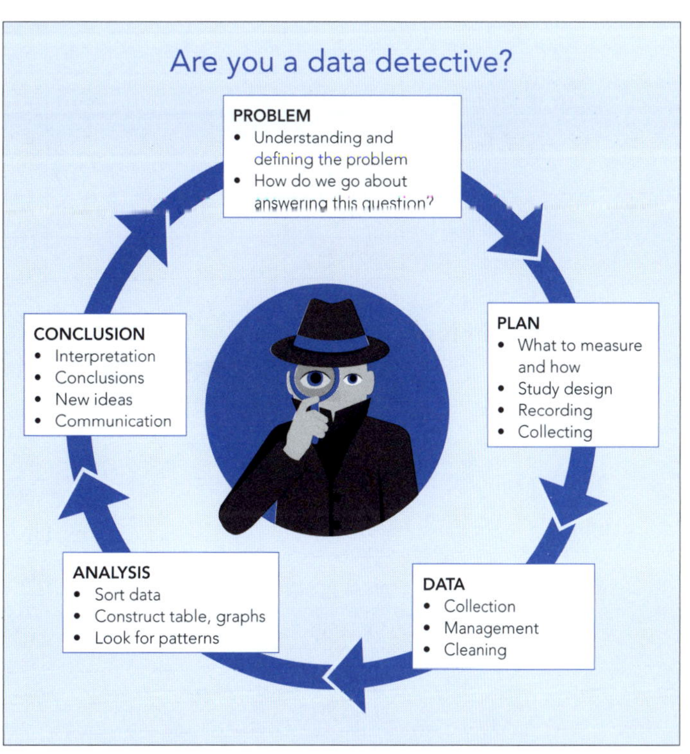

ISBN: 9780170472975

What does the data look like?

- Your data could be in days, weeks, months, quarters or years.

Here are some examples (usually data sets will be larger).

The records of deaths in New Zealand

Time	Male deaths	Female deaths	Total deaths
2020Q1	4116	3861	7977
2020Q2	4176	3906	8082
2020Q3	4431	3960	8391
2020Q4	4221	3999	8220
2021Q1	4191	4053	8244
2021Q2	4494	4125	8619
2021Q3	4836	4686	9522
2021Q4	4500	4080	8580

This data is quarterly.

Quarter 1 is January, February and March.

Quarter 2 is April, May and June.

Quarter 3 is July, August and September.

Quarter 4 is October, November and December.

Food-borne illnesses in New Zealand

Time	Campylobacteriosis	Salmonellosis
2020M11	688	59
2020M12	860	61
2021M01	680	87
2021M02	429	83
2021M03	407	78
2021M04	324	85
2021M05	279	57
2021M06	332	50
2021M07	340	44
2021M08	376	32
2021M09	441	42
2021M10	469	35
2021M11	756	56
2021M12	903	62

This data is monthly.

Unless you are told otherwise, assume M01 is January.

Crimes in New Zealand

Time	Crime
Week1D7	70875
Week2D1	63828
Week2D2	62433
Week2D3	66833
Week2D4	68333
Week2D5	75092
Week2D6	76174
Week2D7	67016

This data is weekly.

Unless you are told otherwise, assume D1 is Monday.

  ISBN: 9780170472975

Features of a times series

- Your graphing program will produce some graphs similar to below.
- You are required to analyse the trend, seasonality and the forecasts.

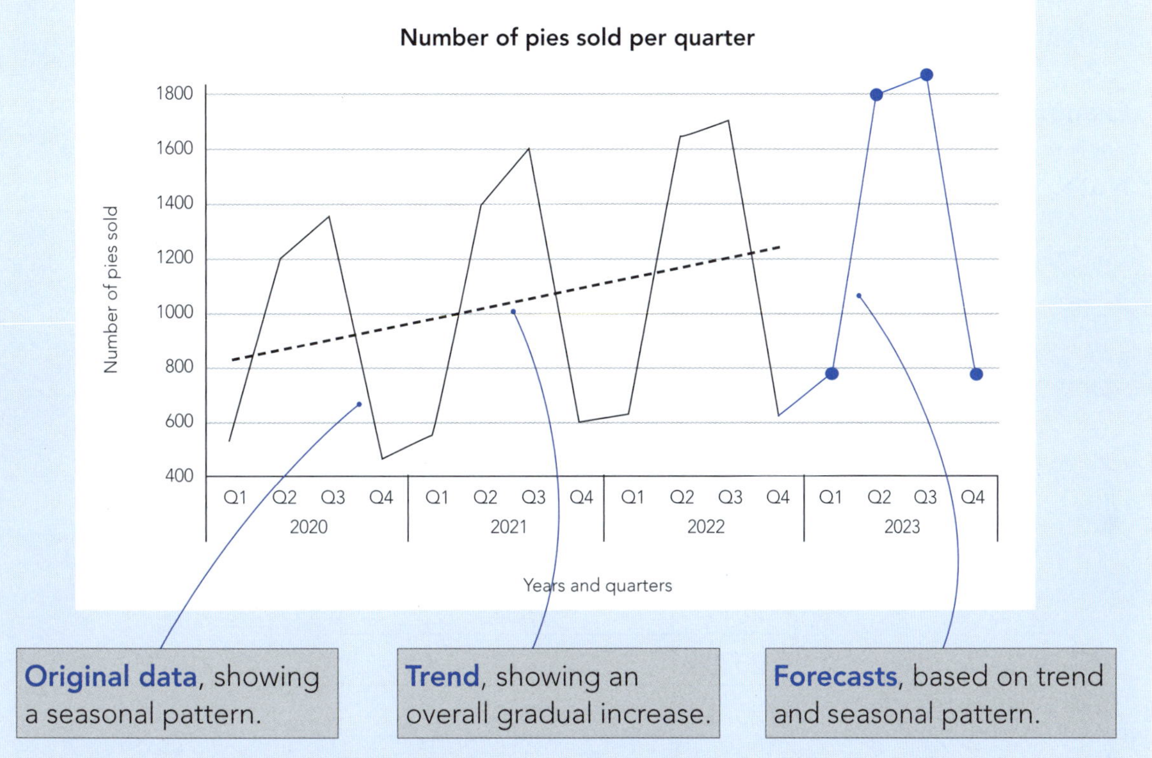

Depending on the computer program you are using, you may have several graphs to analyse and discuss.

ISBN: 9780170472975

The mathematics behind time series

- Most computer programs will graph all the features of a time series for you.
- However, you will be able to write a much better report if you understand some of the mathematics behind time series.

Example: Records have been kept over the last nine years for the number of pies sold each year by the school canteen.
Note: You will usually be given a much bigger data set than this.

Year	Number of pies sold
2013	2690
2014	3094
2015	3751
2016	3631
2017	3612
2018	3871
2019	3545
2020	4125
2021	4607

Plot the data and **think** about it.

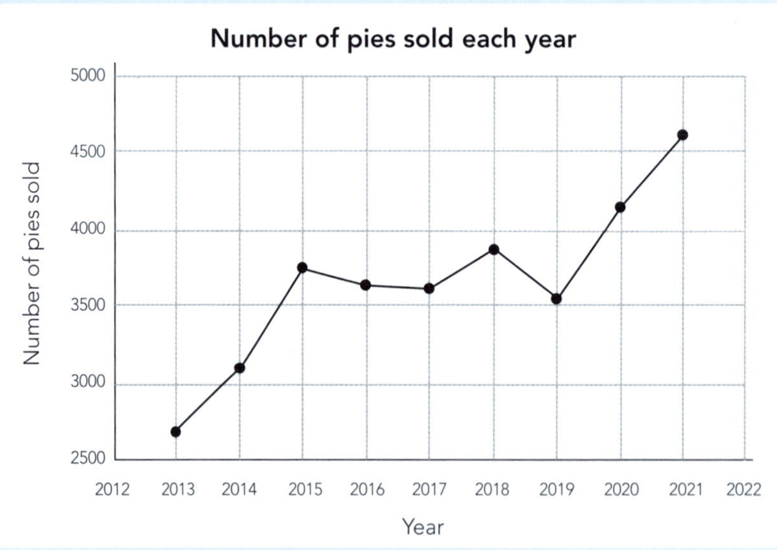

Notice:

1. Overall the number of pies sold per year appears to be increasing.
2. The number of pies sold each year does not increase by a regular number, and during several years it decreases.

We call the overall change the **trend**.

You will need to analyse the trend.

 ISBN: 9780170472975

The trend

Moving means

Three-point moving means

In order to smooth out the data to show the **trend**, we calculate 'moving means' for every group of three years, and write the moving mean beside the **middle** year of each group.

Year	Number of pies sold	Working and moving mean	Trend (year, moving mean)
2013	2690		
2014	3094	$\frac{2690 + 3094 + 3751}{3} = 3178$	(2014, 3178)
2015	3751	$\frac{3094 + 3751 + 3631}{3} = 3492$	(2015, 3492)
2016	3631	$\frac{3751 + 3631 + 3612}{3} = 3665$	(2016, 3665)
2017	3612		(2017, 3705)
2018	3871		(2018, 3676)
2019	3545		
2020	4125		
2021	4607		

Fill in the unshaded cells in the table.

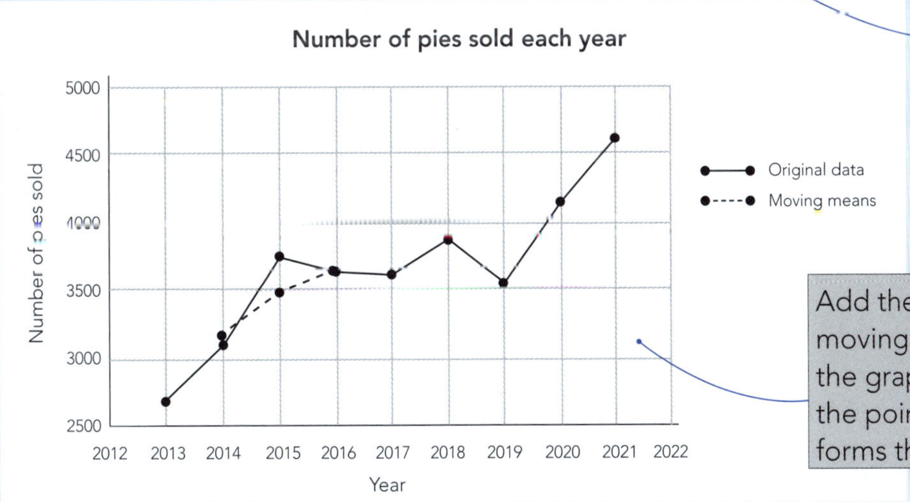

Number of pies sold each year

Original data
Moving means

Add the remaining moving means to the graph, and join the points. This forms the **trend**.

Notice:

1. The moving mean (trend) graph is **smoother** than the original data.
2. The moving means for 2013 and 2021 cannot be calculated using this method. Most computer programs have other ways of finding these.
3. Each of the moving means appears in line with the **middle** of the **three** values used in its calculation.

ISBN: 9780170472975

Four-point moving means

Example: Records have also been kept for the last three years of the numbers of pies sold each **quarter** by the school canteen.

Time series data is recorded at regular intervals, often monthly or quarterly.

Q1 includes January, February and March.

Q4 includes October, November and December.

Year	Quarter	Number of pies sold per quarter
2019	Q1	528
	Q2	1192
	Q3	1360
	Q4	465
2020	Q1	537
	Q2	1379
	Q3	1617
	Q4	592
2021	Q1	625
	Q2	1651
	Q3	1709
	Q4	622

Plot the data and **think** about it.

Notice:

1. Overall the number of pies sold appears to be increasing slightly.
2. There is a repeating pattern.

We call the overall change the **trend**.

You will need to analyse both of these.

We call the repeating pattern the **seasonal pattern**.

 ISBN: 9780170472975

The trend

- We need to calculate moving means of **four**. This ensures that we have just one of each different section of the year in our calculation.
- This causes a problem: if we place our first moving mean in the middle of the four pieces of data that contributed to it, it lies **between** Q2 and Q3.
- The solution is to calculate a **centred moving mean** of two. This is the mean of the first two moving means, which will line up with Q3.

Year	Quarter	Number of pies sold	Working	Moving mean (4)	Working	Centred moving mean (CMM)	Trend (year, CMM)
2019	Q1	528					
	Q2	1192					
			$= \frac{528 + 1192 + 1360 + 465}{4}$	886.25			
	Q3	1360			$\frac{886.25 + 888.5}{2}$	887	(2019 Q3, 887)
			$= \frac{1192 + 1360 + 465 + 537}{4}$	888.5			
	Q4	465			$\frac{888.5 + 935.25}{2}$	912	(2019 Q4, 912)
			$= \frac{1360 + 465 + 537 + 1379}{4}$	935.25			
2020	Q1	537			$\frac{935.25 + 999.5}{2}$	967	(2020 Q1, 967)
				999.5			
	Q2	1379			$\frac{999.5 + 1031.25}{2}$	1015	(2020 Q2, 1015)
				1031.25			

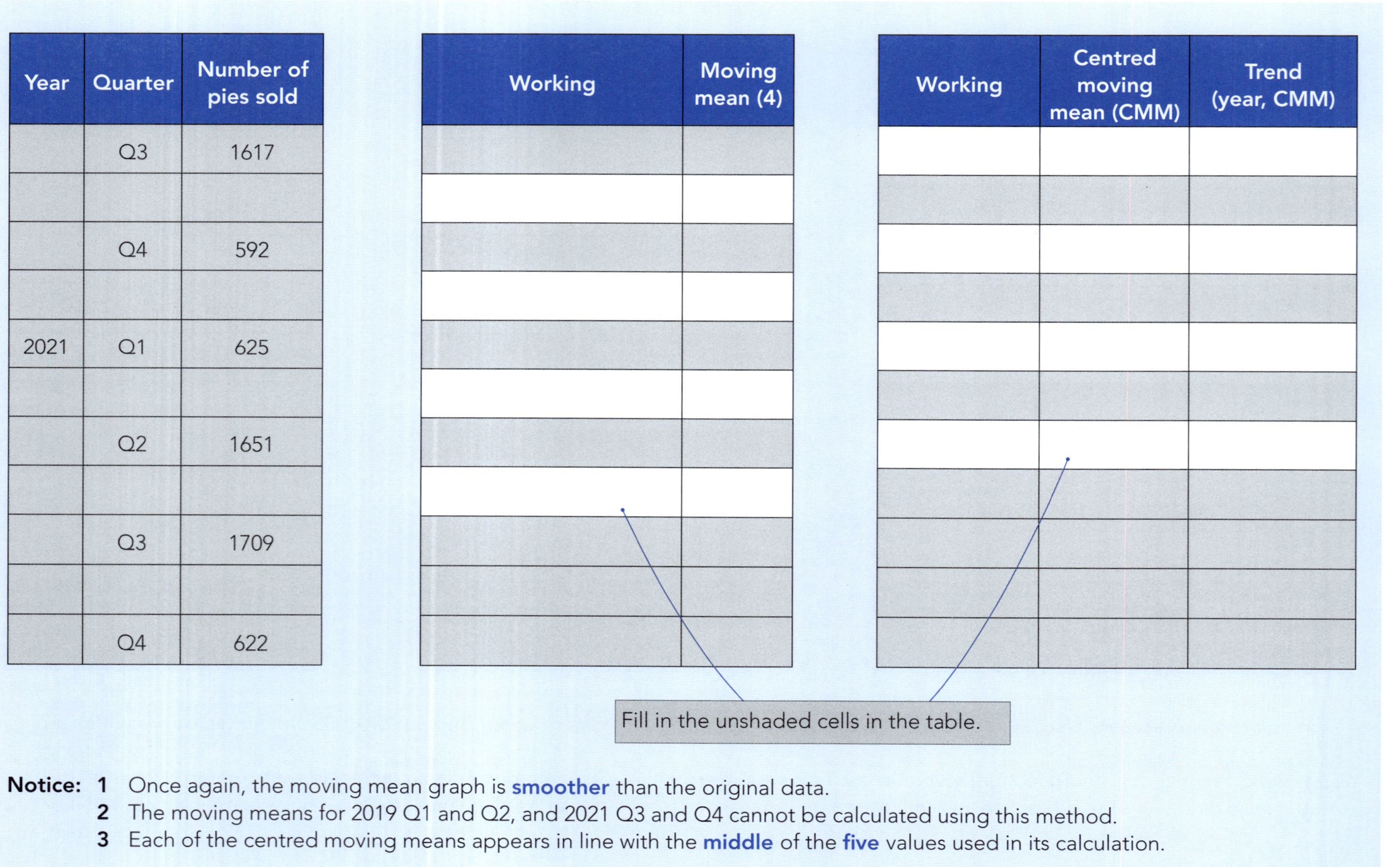

Year	Quarter	Number of pies sold	Working	Moving mean (4)	Working	Centred moving mean (CMM)	Trend (year, CMM)
	Q3	1617					
	Q4	592					
2021	Q1	625					
	Q2	1651					
	Q3	1709					
	Q4	622					

Fill in the unshaded cells in the table.

Notice: **1** Once again, the moving mean graph is **smoother** than the original data.
2 The moving means for 2019 Q1 and Q2, and 2021 Q3 and Q4 cannot be calculated using this method.
3 Each of the centred moving means appears in line with the **middle** of the **five** values used in its calculation.

ISBN: 9780170472975

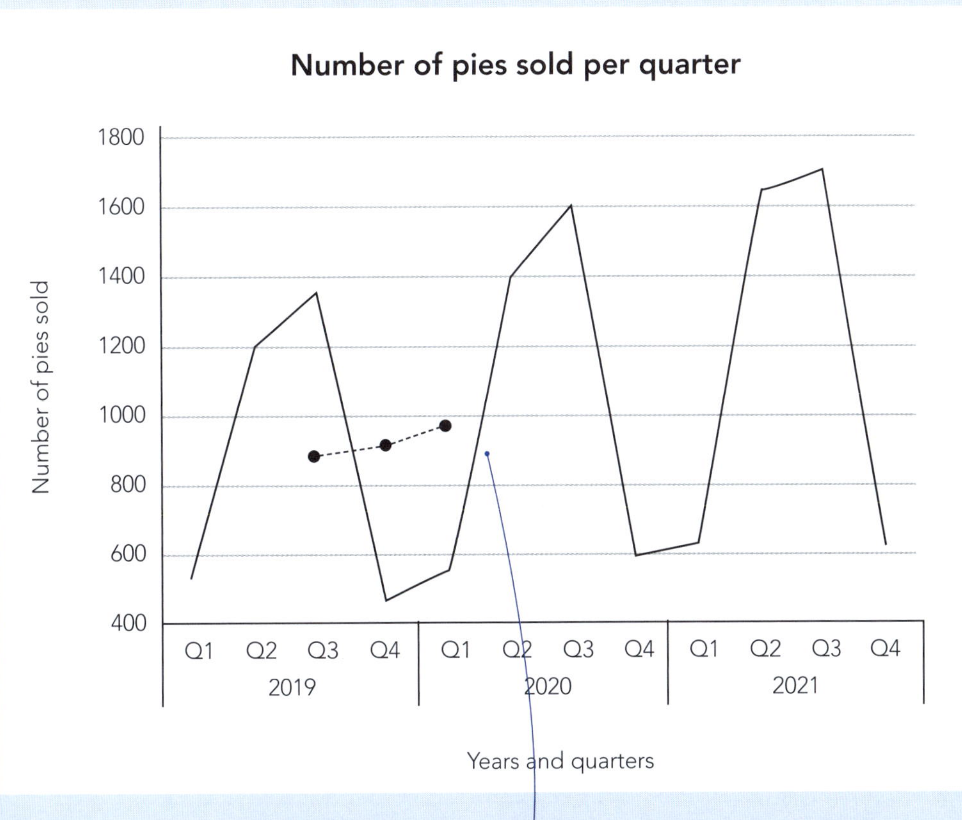

Add the remaining centred moving means to the graph, and join the points. This forms the **trend**.

Notice:
1. Once again, the moving mean graph is **smoother** than the original data.
2. The moving means for the first and last two quarters cannot be calculated using this method. Most computer programs fit a line to the centred moving means, and extend this to cover the ends.
3. Each of the moving means appears in line with the **middle** of the **five** values used in its calculation.

The (centred) moving means form the trend.

The seasonal pattern

Once again, consider the quarterly sales of pies over the last three years.

The seasonal effect for each quarter = raw data value – centred moving mean (CMM)

Year	Quarter	Number of pies sold	CMM	Working	Individual seasonal effect
2019	Q1	528			
	Q2	1192			
	Q3	1360	887	1360 – 887	473
	Q4	465	912	465 – 912	–447
2020	Q1	537	967		–430
	Q2	1379	1015		
	Q3	1617	1042		
	Q4	592	1087		
2021	Q1	625	1133		
	Q2	1651	1148		
	Q3	1709			
	Q4	622			

Fill in the unshaded cells in the table.

Notice that seasonal effects for the first and last two quarters cannot be calculated using this method.

We then use the individual seasonal effects to calculate the **average seasonal effects**:

Season	Working	Average seasonal effect
Q1	$\frac{(-430) + (-508)}{2}$	–469
Q2	$\frac{364 + 503}{2}$	434
Q3		
Q4		

= Average of the individual seasonal effects for **both the first quarters**. This means that during the first quarter, the number of pies sold was 469 **below** average.

Fill in the unshaded cells in the table.

Most computer programs graph these for you, but do not list their values:

ISBN: 9780170472975

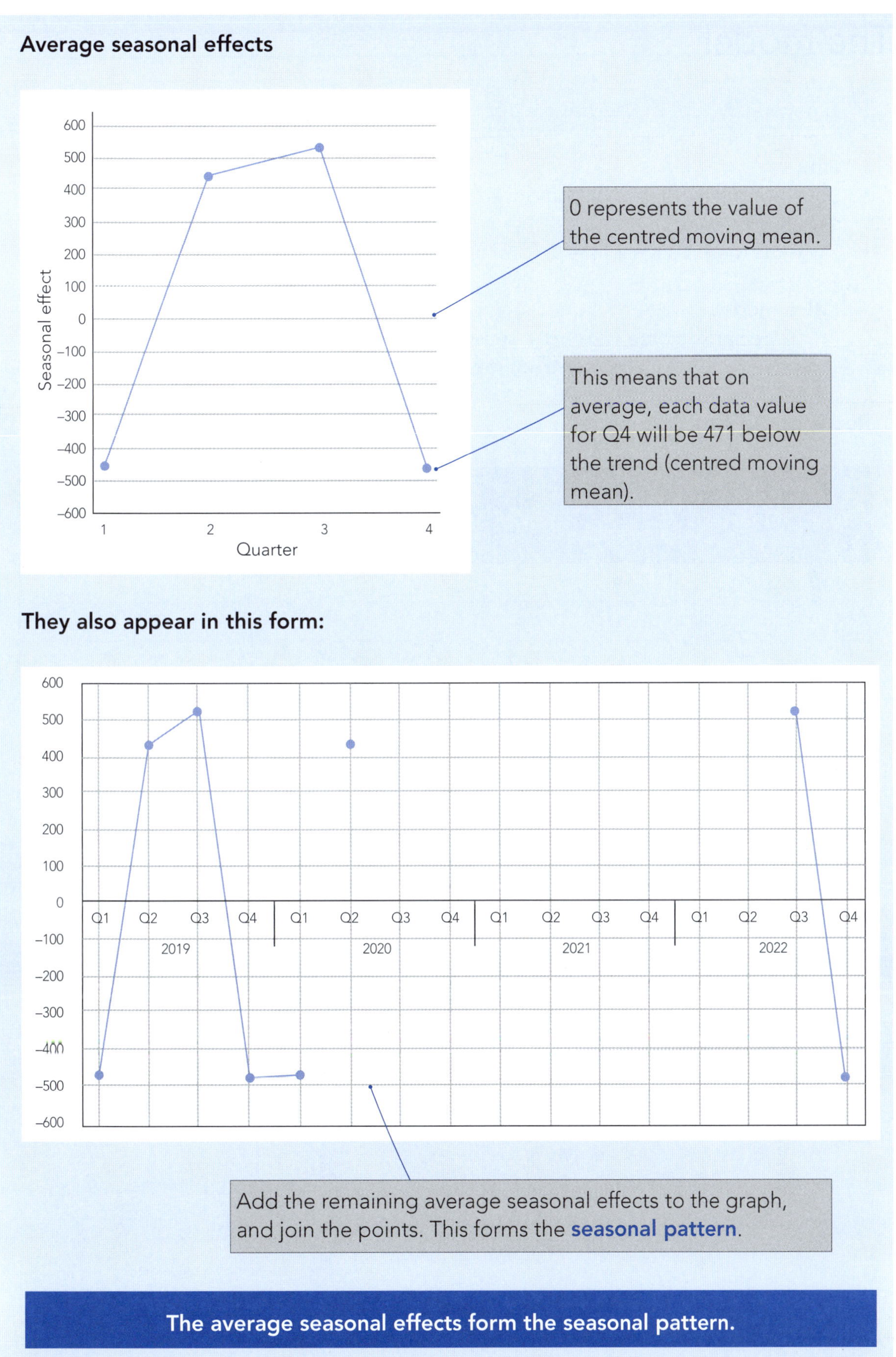
Average seasonal effects
600
500
400
300
200
100
0
–100
–200
–300
–400
–500
–600
Seasonal effect
1
2
3
4
Quarter
0 represents the value of the centred moving mean.
This means that on average, each data value for Q4 will be 471 below the trend (centred moving mean).
They also appear in this form:
Q1
Q2
Q3
Q4
2019
2020
2021
2022
Add the remaining average seasonal effects to the graph, and join the points. This forms the seasonal pattern.
The average seasonal effects form the seasonal pattern.

The model

- In general, we use the **additive** model for time series.
- In many computer programs, the term used for the model values is '**Recomposed data**'.
- Comparing the model or recomposed data with the original data enables us to see any unusual points.
- Once the model is established, **forecasts** can be made.

Additive model:

Time series value = trend + seasonal pattern

= (centred) moving mean + average seasonal effect

Recomposed data (the model):

Year	Quarter	Number of pies sold	CMM	Average seasonal effect	Working	Recomposed data (the model)
2019	Q1	528				
	Q2	1192				
	Q3	1360	887	524	887 + 524	1411
	Q4	465	912	–471	912 + (–471)	441
2020	Q1	537	967	–469		498
	Q2	1379	1015	434		1449
	Q3	1617	1042	524		
	Q4	592	1087	–471		
2021	Q1	625	1133	–469		
	Q2	1651	1148	434		
	Q3	1709				
	Q4	622				

Notice that using this method the data cannot be recomposed for the first and last two quarters. Most computer programs have other ways of finding these.

Fill in the unshaded cells in the table.

These are the numbers of pies that we expected to be sold, based on the trend and the seasonal pattern.

 ISBN: 9780170472975

This is then shown on a graph along with the trend and the original data.

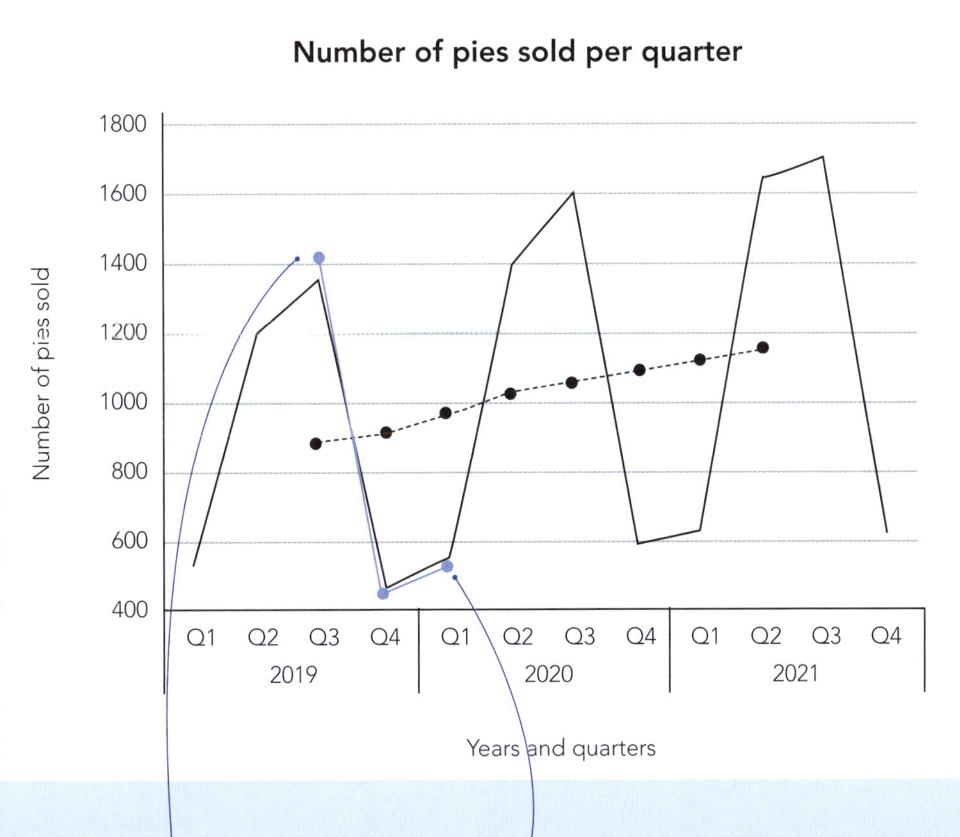

This is the number of pies that we expected to be sold during Q3 of 2019. Notice that the actual number of pies sold was lower. You may or may not be able to find a reason for this.

Add the remaining recomposed data to the graph, and join the points. This forms the **model**.

The trend + the average seasonal effects form the model.

ISBN: 9780170472975

Forecasts

- These are **estimates** only, so they need to be **rounded** appropriately.
- Forecasts that are close to the last piece of data will be more reliable than those that are further away.
- Most computer programs will calculate these for you, along with 95% confidence limits.

Additive model: **Forecast = extended trend + seasonal pattern**

Year	Quarter	Extended trend	Average seasonal effect	Working	Forecasts
2022	Q1	1281	–469	1281 + (–469)	812
	Q2	1320	434		1754
	Q3	1359	524		
	Q4	1399	–471		

Fill in the unshaded cells in the table.

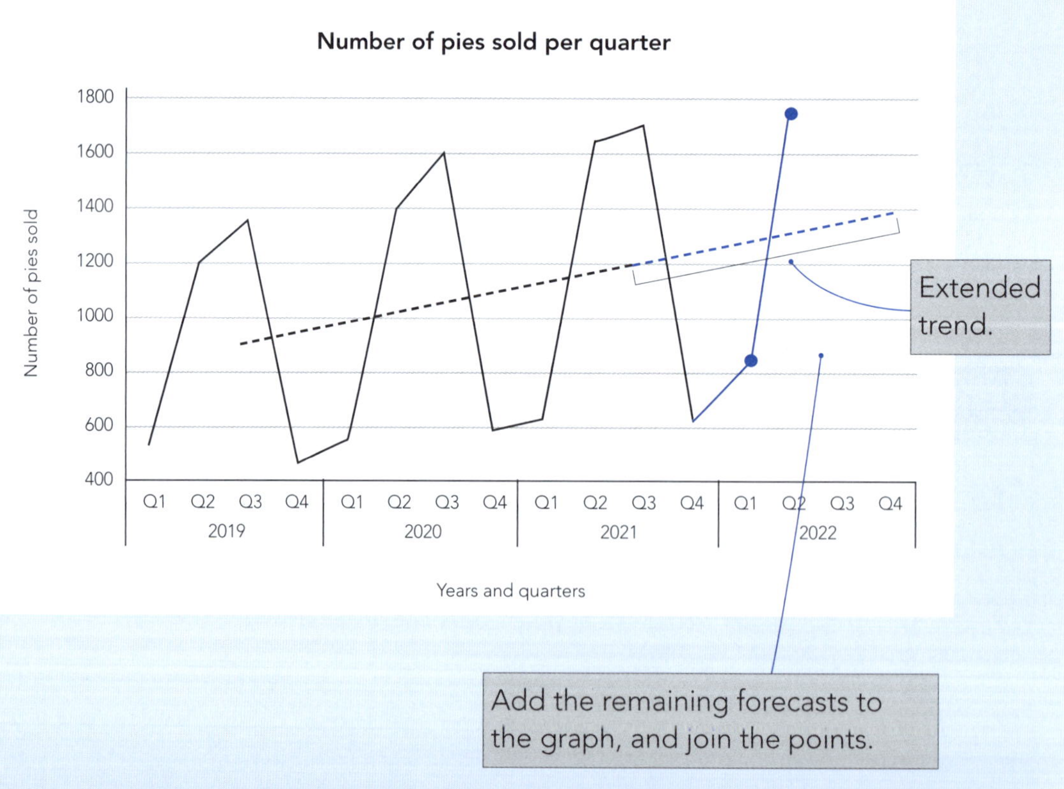

The extended trend + the seasonal pattern form the forecast.

ISBN: 9780170472975

Unusual points

- Time series data is never **exactly** the sum of the trend and the cycle.
- There are always small irregularities, which are often impossible to explain.
- The irregularities are graphed by most computer programs, and are called **residuals**.
- However, at times there are residuals that are large enough to be considered as **unusual points**.
- When these occur, you need to do some **research** and try to find an explanation.

Residual = actual value – model value
= actual value – (trend + average seasonal effect)

Residuals:

Actual number of pies sold.

Number of pies that were expected to be sold.

Year	Quarter	Number of pies sold	CMM	Average seasonal effect	Working	Residuals
2019	Q1	528				
	Q2	1192				
	Q3	1360	887	524	1360 – (887 + 524)	–51
	Q4	465	912	–471	465 – (912 + (–471))	24
2020	Q1	537	967	–469		39
	Q2	1379	1015	434		–70
	Q3	1617	1042	524		
	Q4	592	1087	–471		
2021	Q1	625	1133	–469		
	Q2	1651	1148	434		
	Q3	1709				
	Q4	622				

Fill in the unshaded cells in the table.

The number of pies sold was 51 fewer than expected.

Deciding whether a point is unusual:

- A point is considered unusual if it lies beyond the lines that mark **±10% of the overall spread**.
- Lines representing these thresholds are marked on the residual graph in some computer programs.

Calculation of the threshold:

$$\text{Threshold} = \pm\frac{\text{highest value} - \text{lower value}}{10}$$

For the pie sales:

$$\text{Threshold} = \pm\frac{1709 - 465}{10} = \pm 124$$

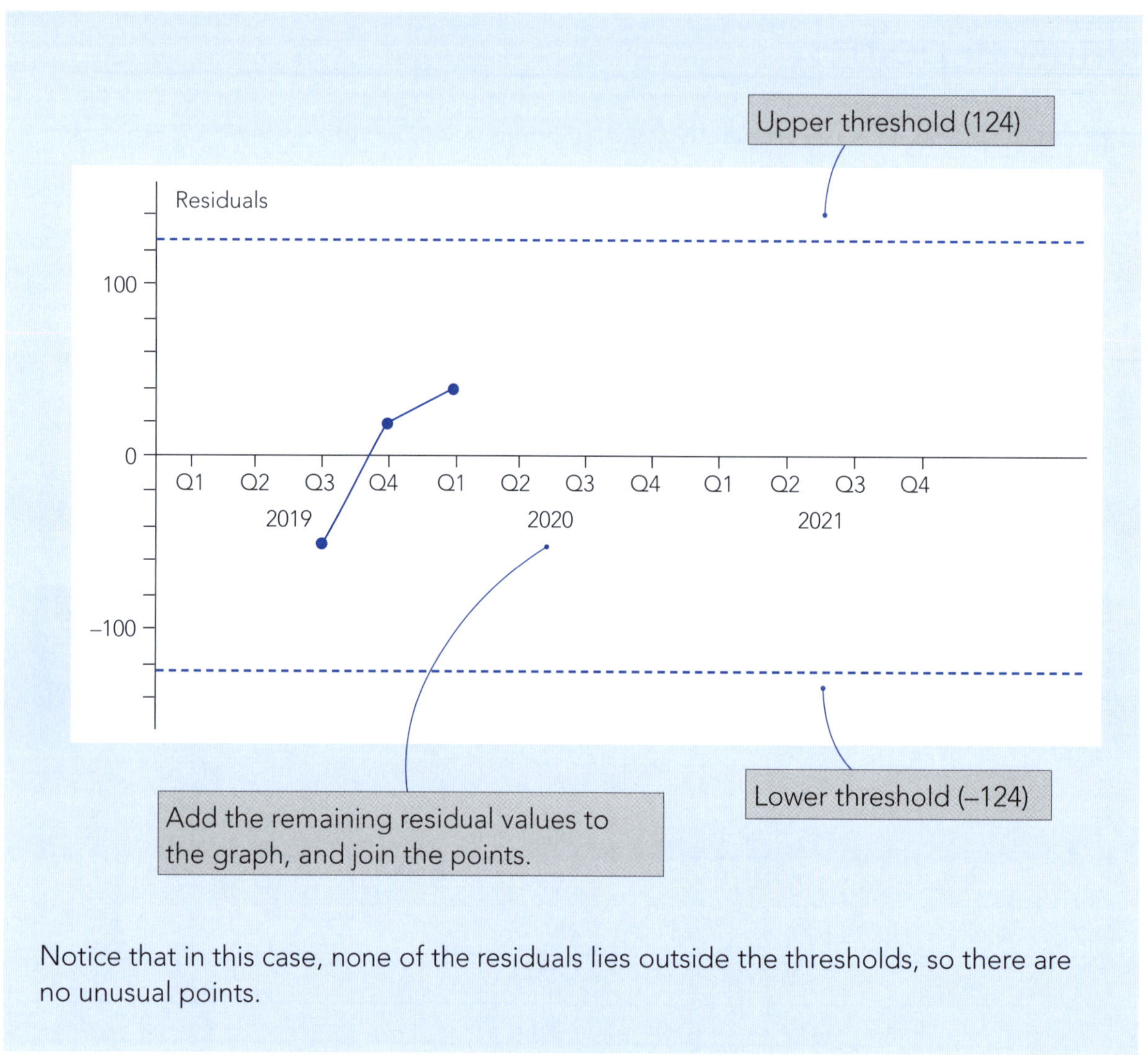

Notice that in this case, none of the residuals lies outside the thresholds, so there are no unusual points.

ISBN: 9780170472975

Requirements of a basic report

You must:

1 Research your context

2 Select a suitable variable that is informed by contextual knowledge

3 State the purpose of your investigation and who would find it useful

4 Describe and quantify the trend

5 Describe and quantify the seasonal pattern

6 Make a forecast in context

7 Communicate your findings in a conclusion.

1 Research your context

- Any statistical analysis should be undertaken alongside research and relevant contextual knowledge.
- Your variable selection and purpose should be informed by this contextual knowledge.
- You must reference your research. Be careful to use legitimate websites.

1 **a** If you were given the food-borne illness data from page 6, what information would you need to know to research before using it?

____

____

____

____

b If you were given the deaths in New Zealand data from page 6, what information would you need to know to research before using it?

____

____

____

____

ISBN: 9780170472975

2 Select a suitable variable that is informed by contextual knowledge

You will be given more data than you need. You should:

- Do some **research** around the topic.
- **Select suitable data** for your investigation:
  - — One of your variables **must** be **time**, which is recorded at **regular intervals**.
  - — It should show a **seasonal pattern**.
  - — It should have the **scope** for discussion, further research and perhaps suggestions for further study.

Be aware: Your choice of data and the quality of your purpose may affect the potential depth of, and therefore the standard of, your final report.

Examples

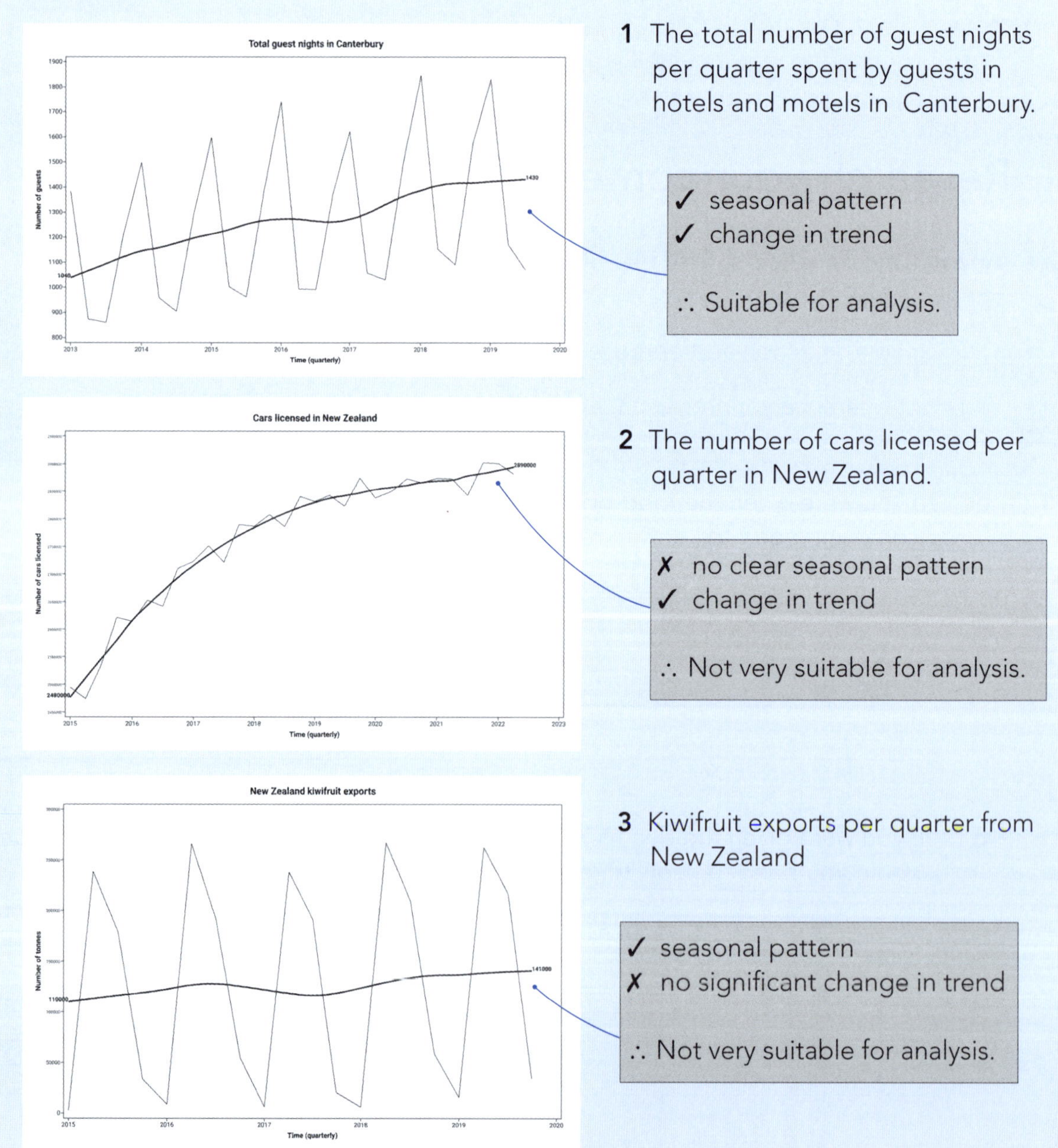

1 The total number of guest nights per quarter spent by guests in hotels and motels in Canterbury.

✓ seasonal pattern
✓ change in trend

∴ Suitable for analysis.

2 The number of cars licensed per quarter in New Zealand.

✗ no clear seasonal pattern
✓ change in trend

∴ Not very suitable for analysis.

3 Kiwifruit exports per quarter from New Zealand

✓ seasonal pattern
✗ no significant change in trend

∴ Not very suitable for analysis.

ISBN: 9780170472975

Are these data sets appropriate for analysing? What might be some potential issues?

1

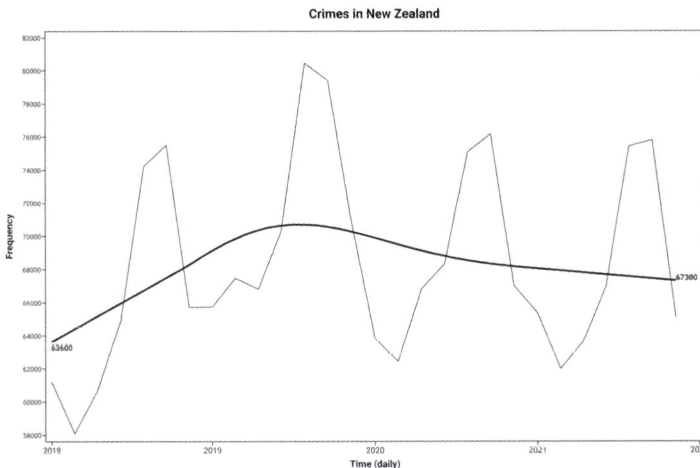

2

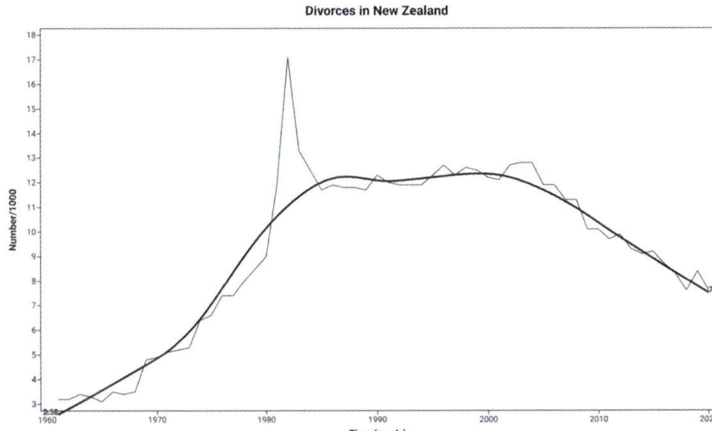

3

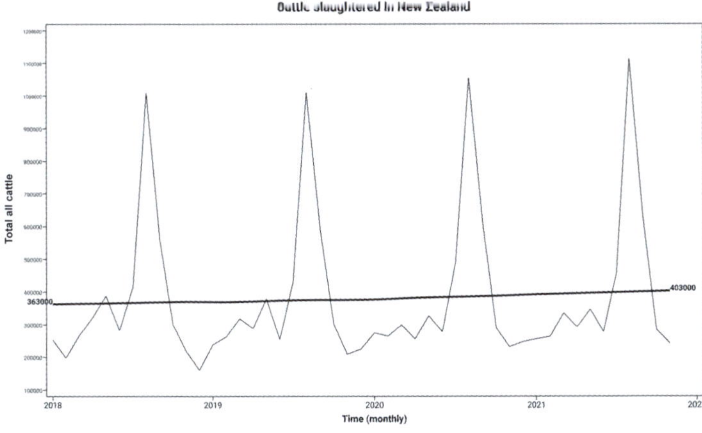

ISBN: 9780170472975

3 State the purpose of your investigation and who would find it useful

- You need to justify why you have chosen your variable.
- You need to discuss who else might be interested in your investigation.
- Do not discuss what you see in your graphs at this stage.
- Discuss any prior research you have done and include references.

Example: Number of deaths in New Zealand.

Why might we investigate this?
The number of deaths occurring is essential (along with data on the numbers of births, new immigrants, and leaving and returning New Zealand residents) for calculating the total population.
It is also important to know the normal death rates so changes due to epidemics, natural disasters, etc. can be accurately assessed.

Who might be interested?
The Department of Statistics, health statisticians, the funeral industry.

Discuss why we might investigate the following issues, who might be interested and what you might research.

1 Kiwifruit are exported from New Zealand around the world.

Why might we investigate this?

____

____

____

____

Who might be interested?

____

____

____

____

What might you research?

____

____

____

____

ISBN: 9780170472975

2 The number of crimes each day in New Zealand.

Why might we investigate this?

Who might be interested?

What might you research?

3 The number of sheep slaughtered in New Zealand throughout the year.

Why might we investigate this?

Who might be interested?

What might you research?

ISBN: 9780170472975

4 The trend

- This is the overall change in the data.
- It is formed by placing a straight line or smooth curve through the moving means.
- This may consist of a steady increase or decrease over the period of the data.
- If there is no overall change, the time series is known as 'stationary'.
- There may also be increases and decreases between the start and the end of the data.

Factors that influence the trend could include:

- demographic changes: shifts in population, changes in population composition, etc.
- economic shifts
- technological changes: new or improved products, etc.
- global factors such as warming, CO_2 levels, movement of currents, etc.

Examples:

1 This shows the total number of nights spent by both domestic (New Zealand) and international guests in hotels and motels in Canterbury from the start of 2017 until quarter 3 in 2021.

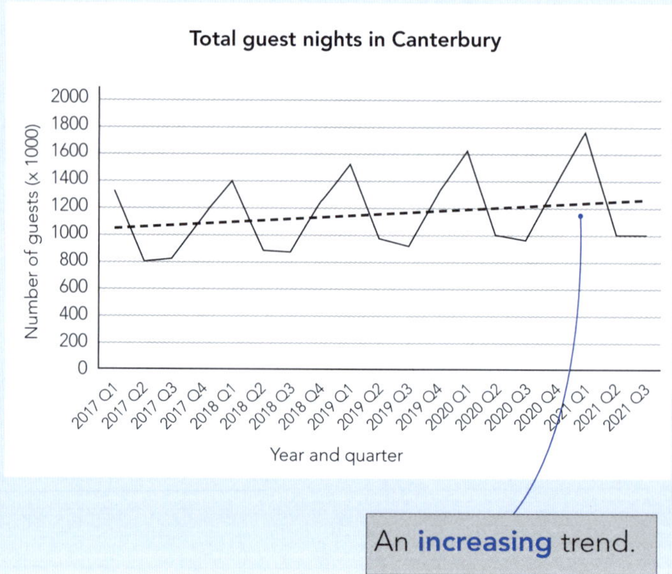

2 This shows the number of invasive pneumococcal disease cases in New Zealand from the start of 2014 until the end of 2020. Invasive pneumococcal disease can cause pneumonia, blood infection, middle ear infection and meningitis.

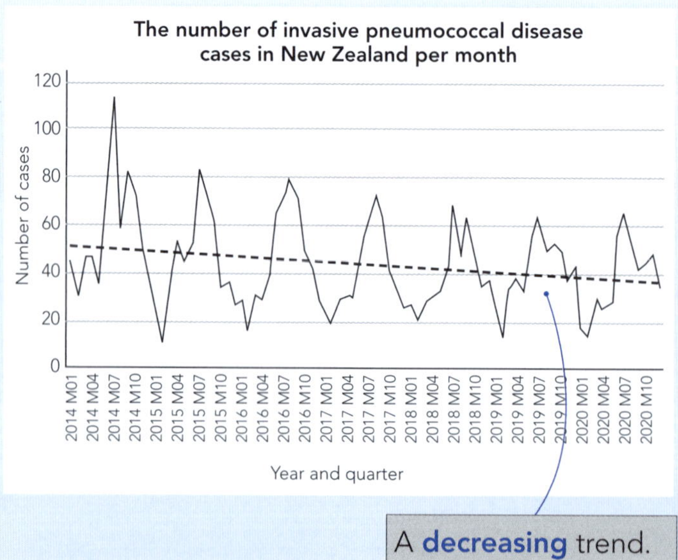

ISBN: 9780170472975

3 This shows the total number of nights spent by both domestic and international guests (combined) in hotels and motels in Canterbury from the start of 2009 until quarter 3 in 2015.

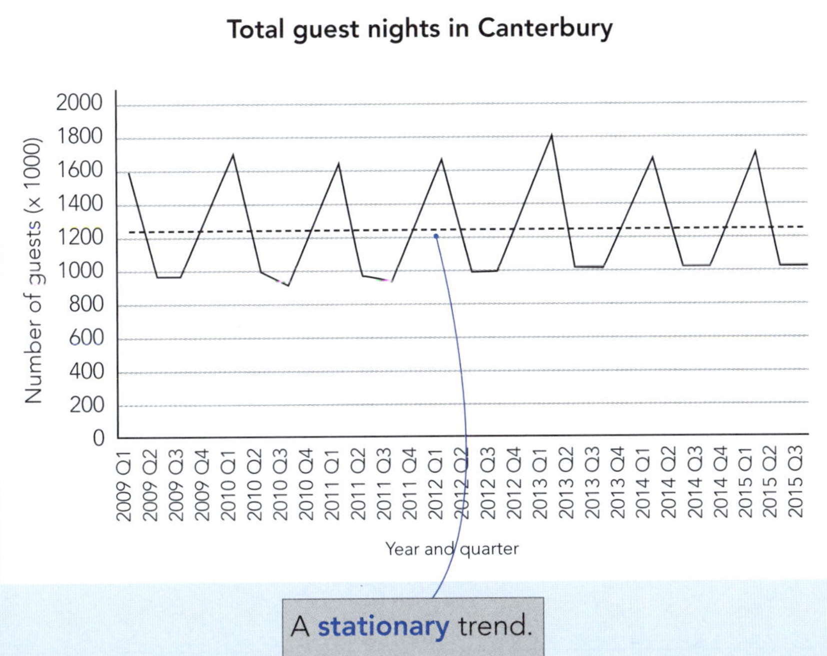

A **stationary** trend.

4 This shows the total number of deaths in New Zealand from the start of 2013 until the third quarter in 2021.

Overall the trend is increasing, but there are **both increases and decreases** between the start and the finish.

ISBN: 9780170472975

Describe and quantify the trend

You need to:

1 Produce a **graph** showing the raw data as well as the trend.

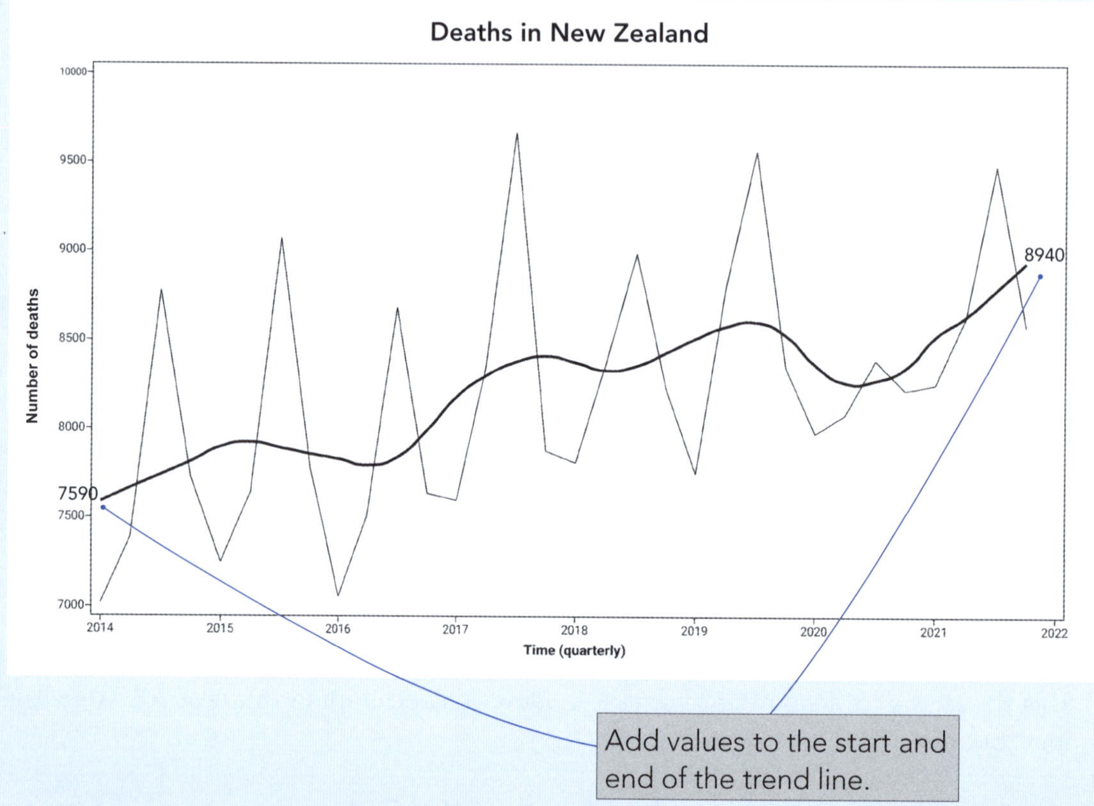

2 Describe and quantify the trend in context, including:

a Stating the overall change in the trend between the start of the data and the end.

e.g. There is an overall ~~decrease~~/**increase** in the trend for the number of deaths in New Zealand from 7590 per *quarter* at the start of 2014 to 8940 per *quarter* in late 2021.

b Describing what happens between the start and the finish.

e.g. Over this period the number of deaths per quarter increases fairly steadily apart from a drop in late 2015 and early 2016, and a significant drop in the first half of 2020.

c Describing what has happened in the most recent data.

e.g. Since mid-2020, the number of deaths has increased steadily.

Don't feel you have to mention every increase and decrease; pick the ones you think are significant. To add depth to your report, you would research to see if you can find any explanations for these increases and decreases.

ISBN: 9780170472975

Describe the trend for each of the following sets of data.

1 The graphs shows the amount of sugar (tonnes) and sugar confectionery imported into New Zealand each month from 2014 until the end of 2021.

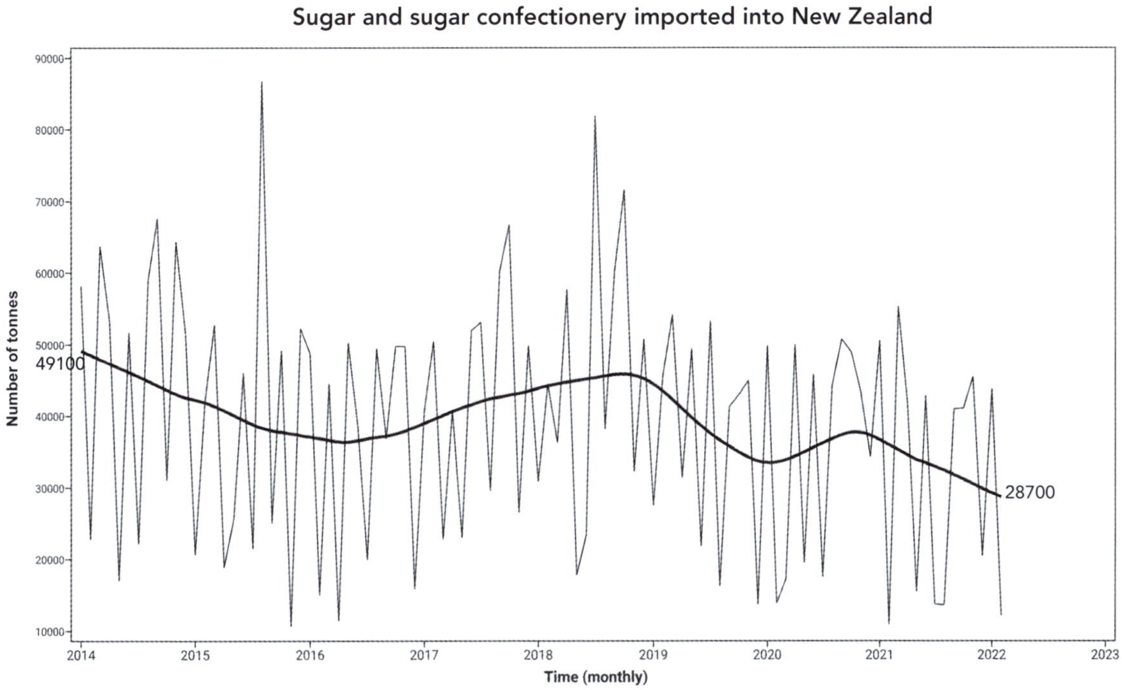

Sugar and sugar confectionery imported into New Zealand

a **Overall change**

There is an overall increase/decrease in the trend for the amount of sugar imported into New Zealand from ____________ per ____________ in ____________ to ____________ per ____________ in ____________.

b **Change between start and finish**

From 2014 until 2019, ____________.

During 2019, ____________.

In 2020, there is a slight ____________ followed by a ____________ during 2021.

c **Most recent data**

During 2021, the data has been ____________.

ISBN: 9780170472975

2 The graph shows the number of births per quarter in New Zealand from 2014 until Q4 in 2021.

Births in New Zealand

Number of births: 17000, 16500, 16000, 15500, 15000, 14500, 14300, 14000, 13500

Time (quarterly): 2014, 2015, 2016, 2017, 2018, 2019, 2020, 2021, 2022

15500

a There is an overall increase/decrease in the trend in births in New Zealand from

_______________ per _______________ in _______________ to _______________ per

_______________ in _______________.

b From 2014 until 2019, ____

____.

From 2019 until mid-2020, ____

____.

c Since mid-2020, the data has been ____.

ISBN: 9780170472975

3 The graph shows the number of pneumococcal cases in New Zealand per month from 2016 until the end of 2021.

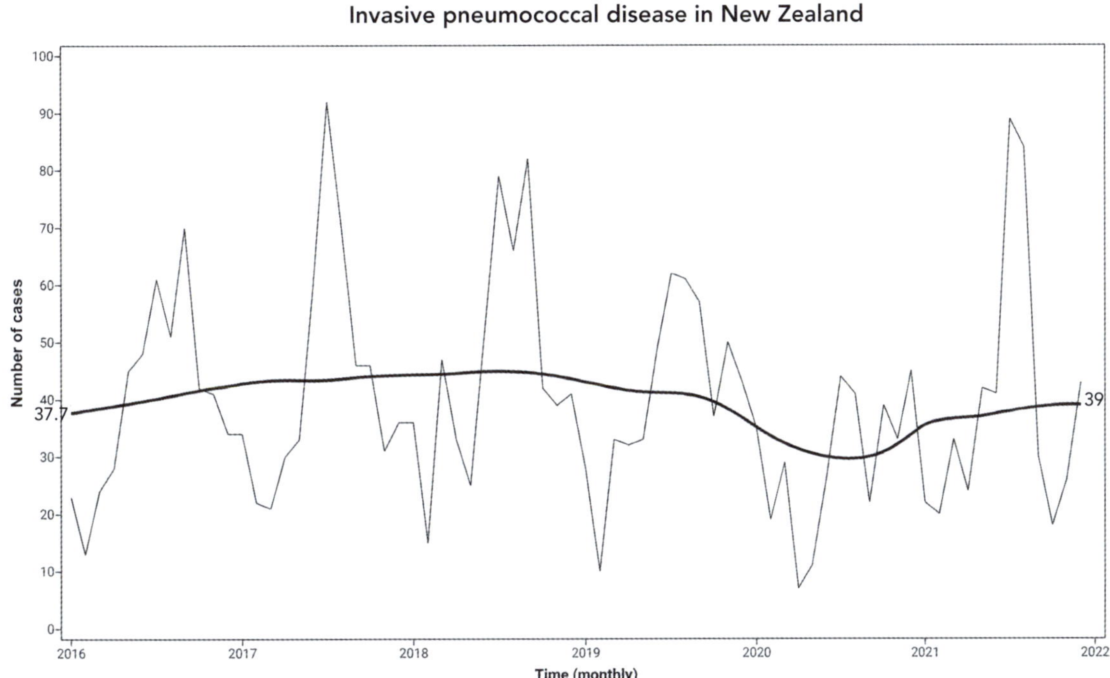

a

b

c

4 The graph shows the number of court proceedings for all offences in New Zealand per month from July 2014 until the end of 2021.

(A proceeding is a legal action initiated against an alleged offender for an offence.)

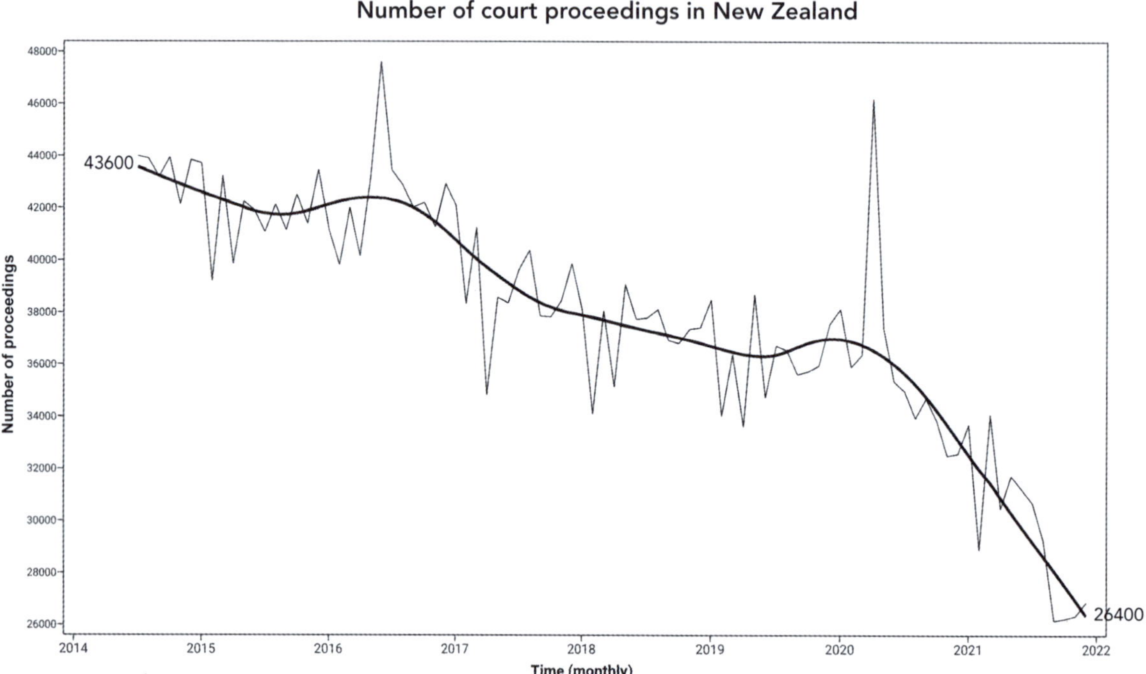

 ISBN: 9780170472975

5 The seasonal pattern

- The seasonal pattern of rises and falls is the result of the influence of 'seasonal' factors.
- Your computer program will calculate and graph the seasonal averages for you.
- It takes all the values for (say) Monday and finds the average value for Mondays. Then it does the same for all the Tuesdays, etc.

The seasonal pattern could be in quarters, months or days. This is determined by the original data set.

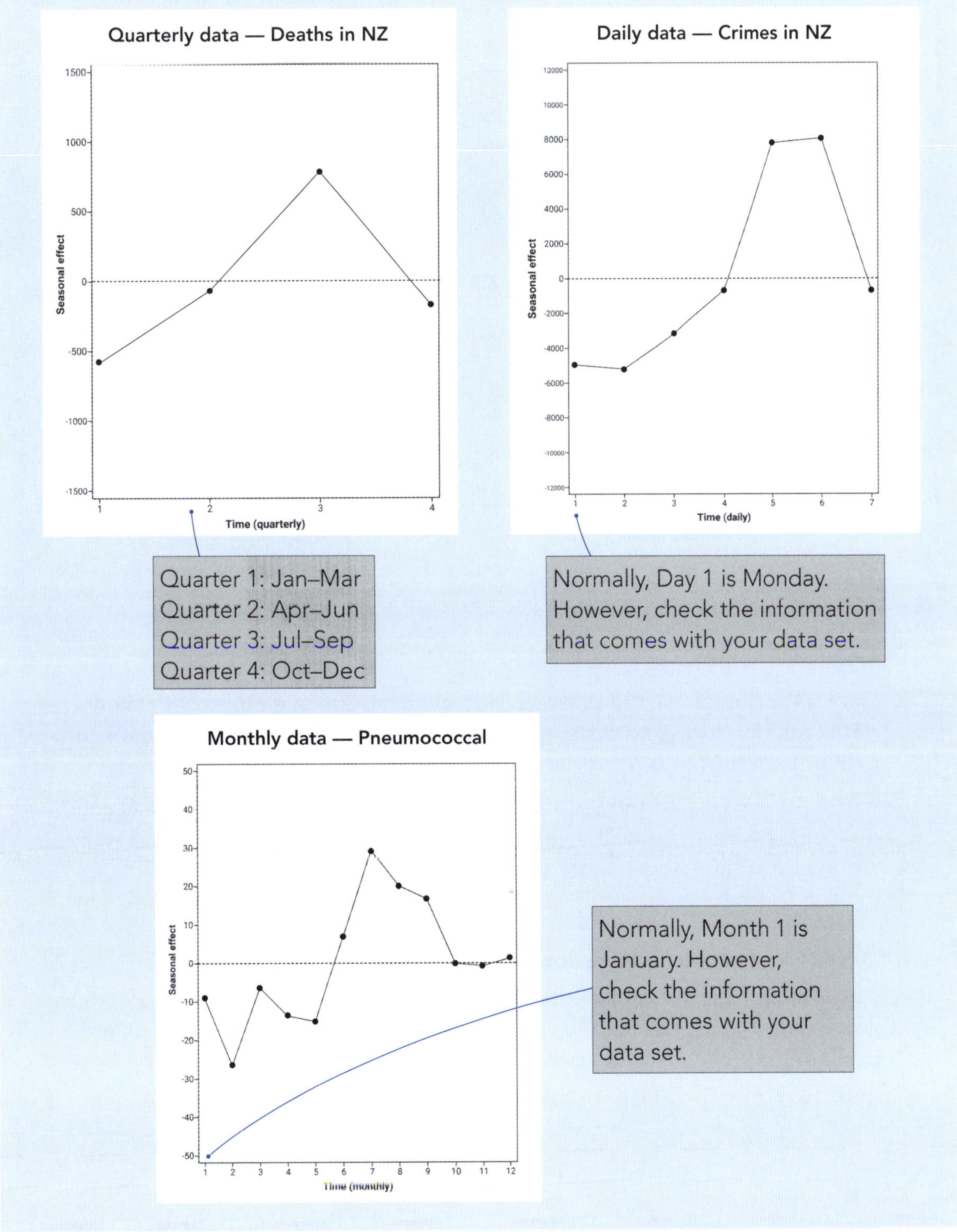

ISBN: 9780170472975

Describe and quantify the seasonal pattern

Example 1:

1 Produce a **graph** showing the average seasonal pattern.
This is the seasonal graph for New Zealand deaths.

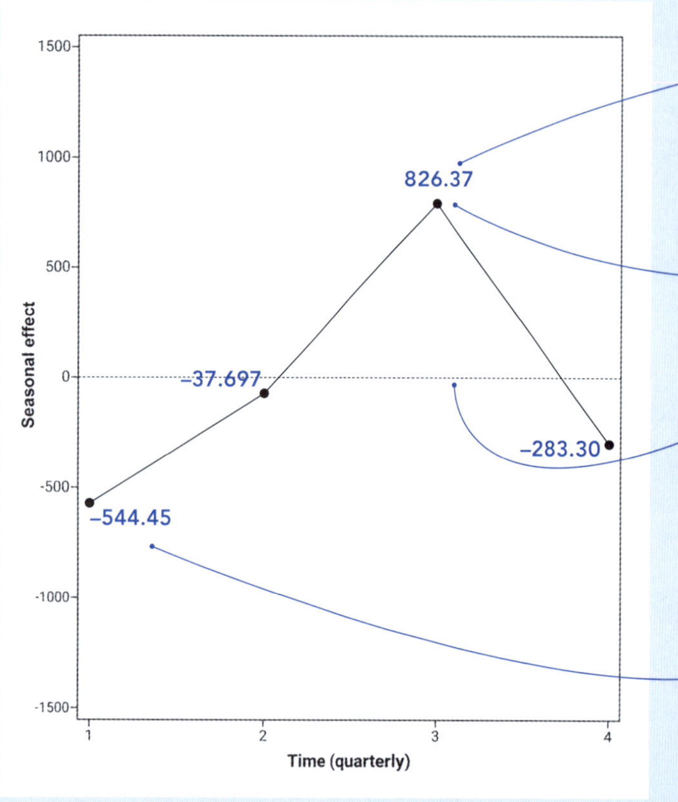

If the variable is **discrete**, you should **round** your data, e.g. in the third quarter there are, on average, 826 deaths.

The values for each 'season' can usually be found by hovering your mouse over the dot.

This line is the average. Any values above it are above-average values, and any values below it are below-average values.

−544.45 means that during the first quarter, the number of deaths is usually about **544 below average**. **DO NOT** use the negative sign and the word 'below' together.

2 **Describe and quantify the seasonal pattern in context, including:**

a **Listing the values for the seasons. However, if you have monthly or daily data, you don't have to state every value. Just pick the important ones, or group them together if they are similar.**

e.g. In the first quarter the deaths are around 544 below average. In the second quarter there are around 38 deaths below average. In the third quarter there are around 826 deaths above average. In the fourth quarter there are around 283 deaths below average.

b **Discussing possible reasons for the overall pattern.**

e.g. The number of deaths per quarter is highest in the third quarter during the winter. Possible reasons for this are greater prevalence of colds, influenza, etc., partly due to low temperatures and also due to easier spread of these because more time is spent indoors.

ISBN: 9780170472975

Example 2:
This is the seasonal graph for the average number of cases of invasive pneumococcal disease in New Zealand. This data is monthly so there are twelve points. Rather than writing about each one, pick some you find significant.

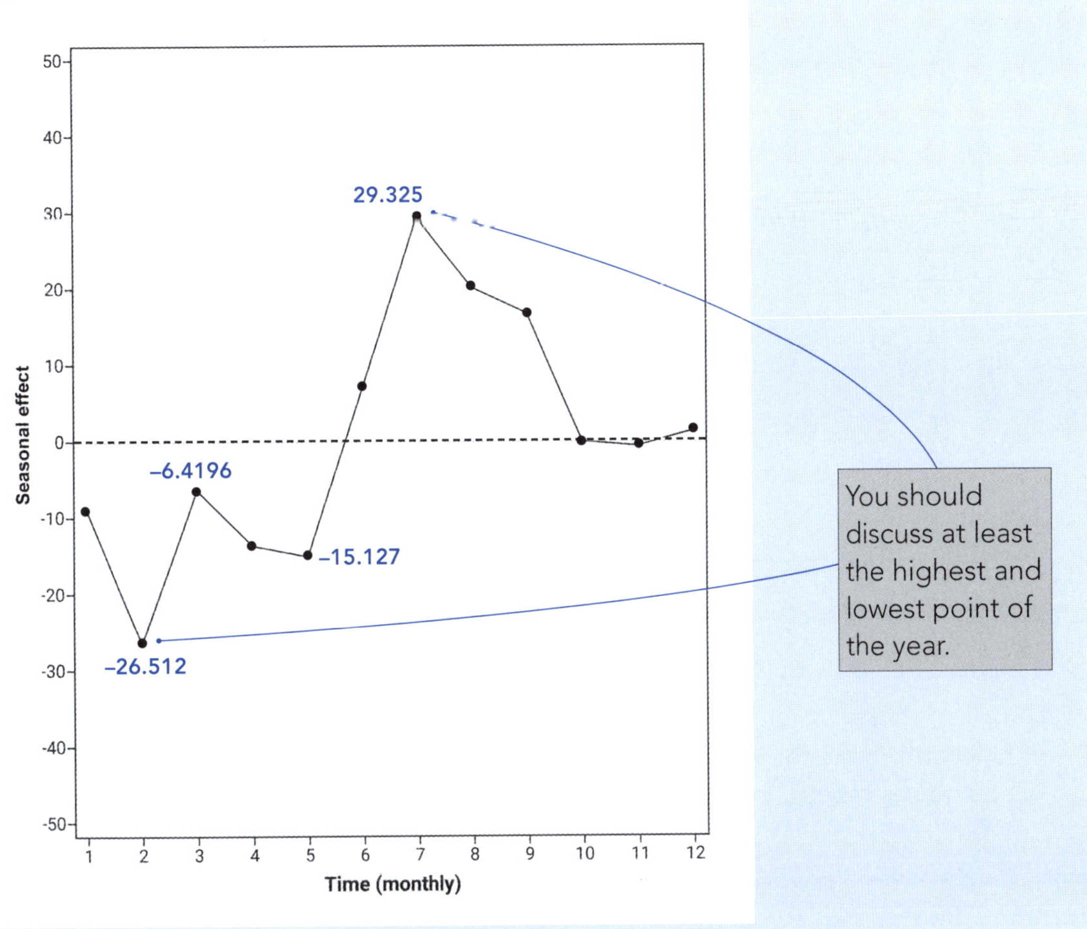

Describe and quantify the seasonal pattern in context.
In February, the number of invasive pneumococcal cases is around 27 below the average. In March, this rises to around 6 cases below the average. By May, it has decreased to around 15 below average. The peak number of cases is in July, with 29 cases above the average.

Discuss possible reasons for the overall pattern.
The number of cases is highest in the months of July, August and September (winter and early spring). Invasive pneumococcal disease is a respiratory disease that is spread to others through direct contact with respiratory secretions, like saliva or mucus. It is likely that the number of cases is higher in winter and early spring because people tend to be inside more and therefore in close contact.

ISBN: 9780170472975

Outline the seasonal patterns and suggest reasons for them where possible.

1 The graph shows the average quantity of apples (tonnes) exported into New Zealand per quarter from 2013 until 2021.

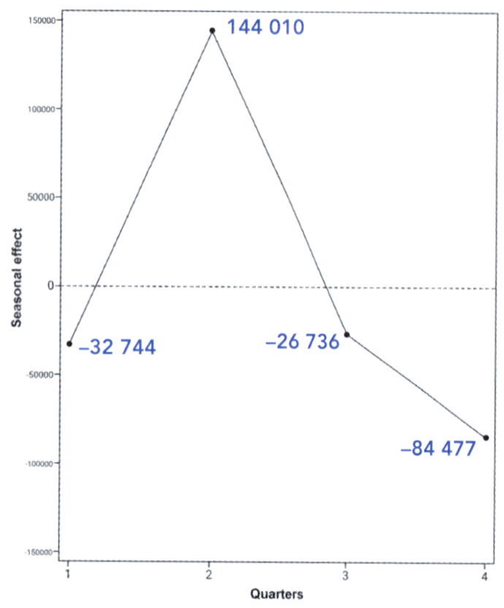

Seasonal pattern:

Quarter 1: There are almost 33 000 tonnes of apples below average exported in Quarter 1.

Quarter 2: ______________________

Quarter 3: ______________________

Quarter 4: ______________________

Reasons: ______________________

2 The graph shows the average number of seasonal cases of salmonellosis in New Zealand per month from 2016 until 2021. Note: You don't have to talk about every month.

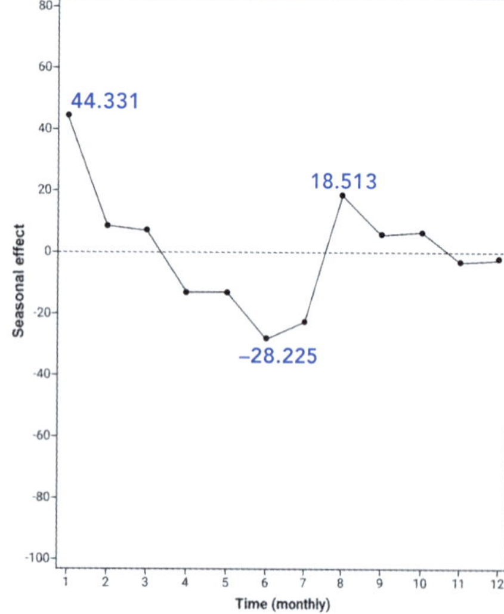

Seasonal pattern:

There is a peak of about __________ __________ above/below average in January.

From then until June, ______________________.

From July to August, ______________________.

From August onwards, ______________________.

Reasons: ______________________

  ISBN: 9780170472975

3 The graph shows the average number of crimes in New Zealand per day from 2018 until 2021.

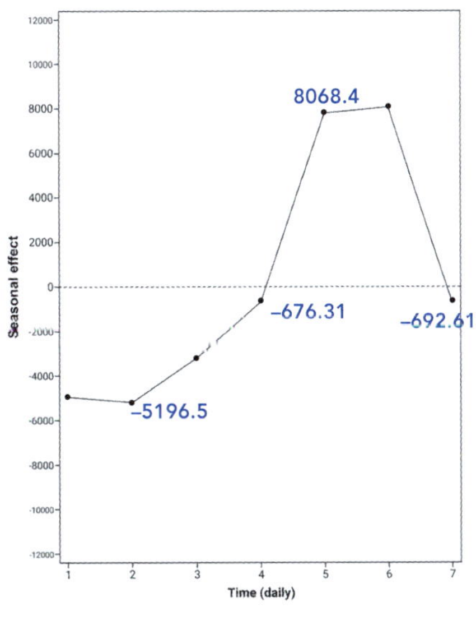

4 The graph shows the seasonal amount of sugar and sugar confectionery (tonnes) imported into New Zealand per month from 2014 until 2021.

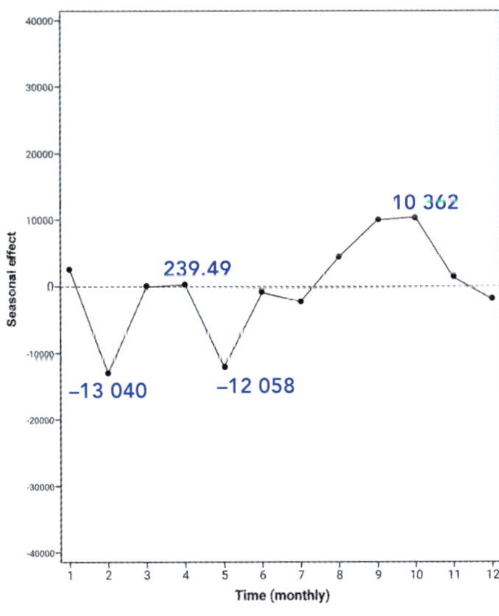

6 Make a forecast in context

- Your computer program will calculate and graph these for you.
- You need to give at least one forecast in context, complete with units and the 95% limits between which it is expected to lie.
- Because we are using mathematical models to describe real situations, we can never be certain that predictions will be accurate. Therefore they should be **rounded** appropriately.
- The underlying assumption in making a forecast is that both the trend and the seasonal pattern will continue unchanged.
- Most programs use exponential smoothing, which means that the most recent values have the greatest impact on predictions.
- How accurate they are will depend on:
  — how well the model fits the data
  — how far in advance is the prediction being made.

Example: The number of deaths per quarter in New Zealand.

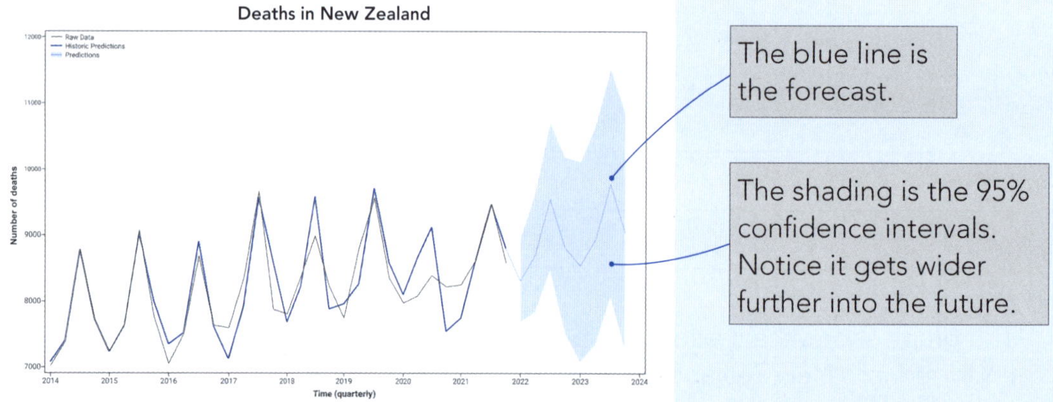

The blue line is the forecast.

The shading is the 95% confidence intervals. Notice it gets wider further into the future.

The table shows the values of the forecasts for each quarter, along with the upper 95% boundary (maximum) and the lower 95% boundary (minimum).

Time	Min	Prediction	Max
2022Q1	7496.9	8185.9	8631.1
2022Q2	7708.6	87.10	9669.2
2022Q3	8320.4	9546.5	10696
2022Q4	7280.2	8661	10038
2023Q1	6810	8297.9	9810.5
2023Q2	7143.6	8822	10498
2023Q3	7756.5	8658.5	11482
2023Q4	6827	8772.9	10631

Note: Due to the method used to calculate predictions and 95% boundaries, the results will vary slightly each time they are calculated.

Include the context.

The number of deaths expected in New Zealand in the first quarter of 2022 is approximately 8186.

Include the word 'about' or 'approximately'.

Include the rounded value and units if appropriate.

Include the time period.

We can be 95% confident that the number of deaths in New Zealand in Quarter 1 of 2022 will be between 7497 and 8631. **Sometimes you will get negative values as forecasts. If this is the case, think carefully about whether it's possible in the given context. If not, then the value should be rounded to 0.**

 ISBN: 9780170472975

Write a sentence describing the forecasts below.

1 Forecasts for the average number of births per quarter in New Zealand.

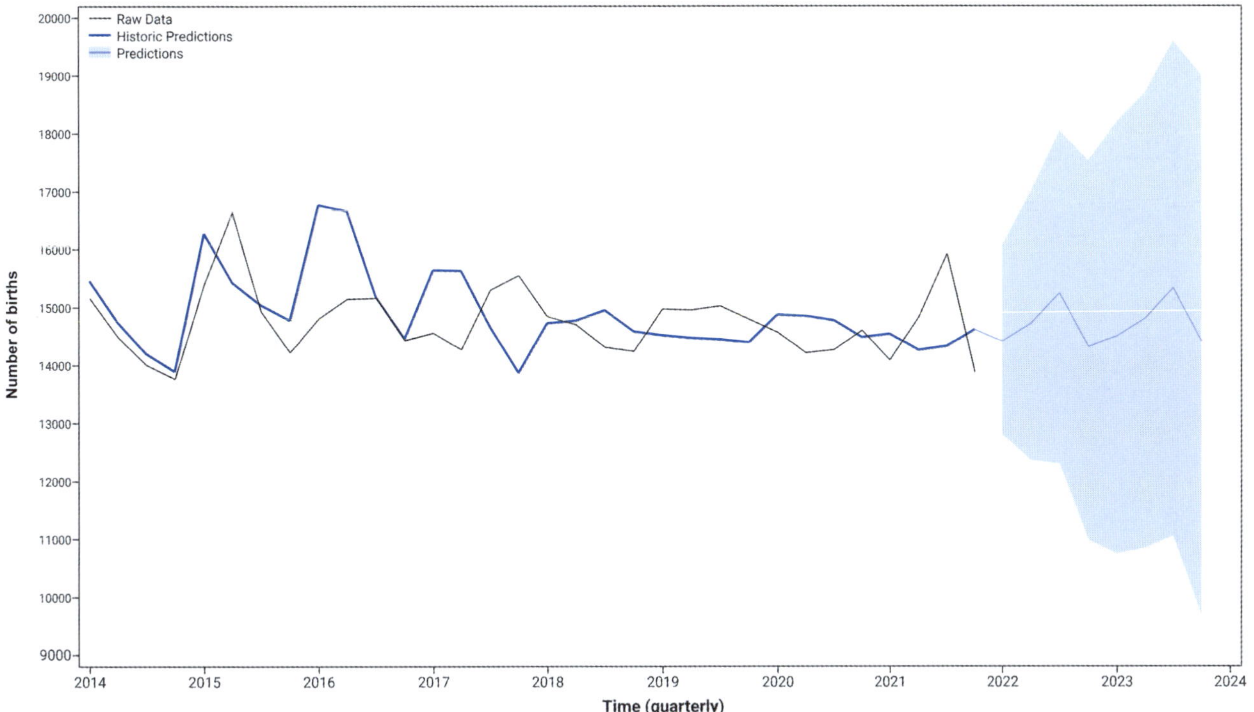

Time	Min	Prediction	Max
2022Q1	13316	14653	15996
2022Q2	12650	14604	16631
2022Q3	12415	14824	17142
2022Q4	11506	14298	17013
2023Q1	11461	14622	17618
2023Q2	10917	14573	17990
2023Q3	10933	14793	18449
2023Q4	10250	14266	18215

The number of births expected in New Zealand in the first quarter of 2022 is approximately ____________________.

We can be 95% confident that the number of births in New Zealand in Quarter 1 of 2022 will be between ________________ and ________________.

ISBN: 9780170472975

2 Forecasts for the average number of court proceedings per month in New Zealand.

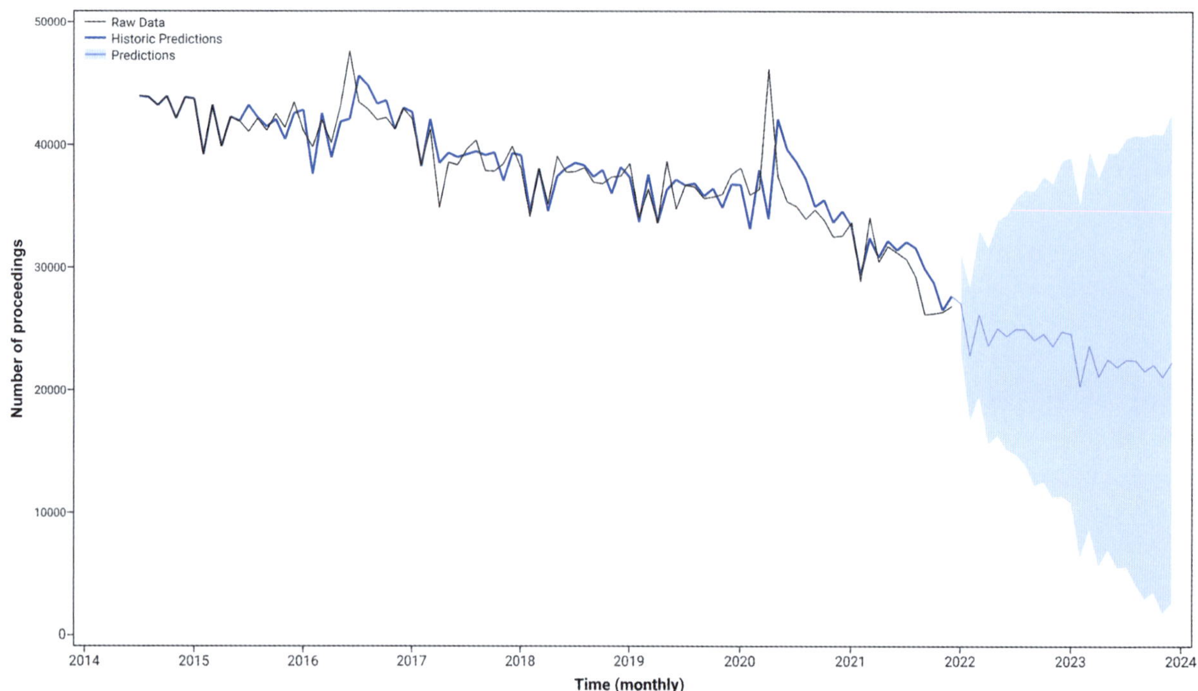

Time	Min	Prediction	Max
2022M01	23163	27096	31077
2022M02	16919	22830	28489
2022M03	19680	26155	33597
2022M04	15968	23628	32236
2022M05	16268	25038	34255
2022M06	14107	24410	34380
2022M07	13649	24990	35750
2022M08	13001	24942	36302
2022M09	12213	24069	35917
2022M10	11919	24595	38281
2022M11	9791	23591	37750
2022M12	10261	24778	39454
2023M01	10192	24579	39796
2023M02	5504.6	20313	36188
2023M03	8165.9	23638	39637
2023M04	4499.3	21111	38099
2023M05	56366.3	22521	39624
2023M06	4488.2	21893	40026
2023M07	4560.6	22473	41086
2023M08	5046.8	22424	40803
2023M09	350032	21552	39721
2023M10	3206.2	22078	40974
2023M11	1847.8	21074	40014
2023M12	2644.7	22261	41619

 ISBN: 9780170472975

3 Forecasts for the average number of crimes per day in New Zealand.

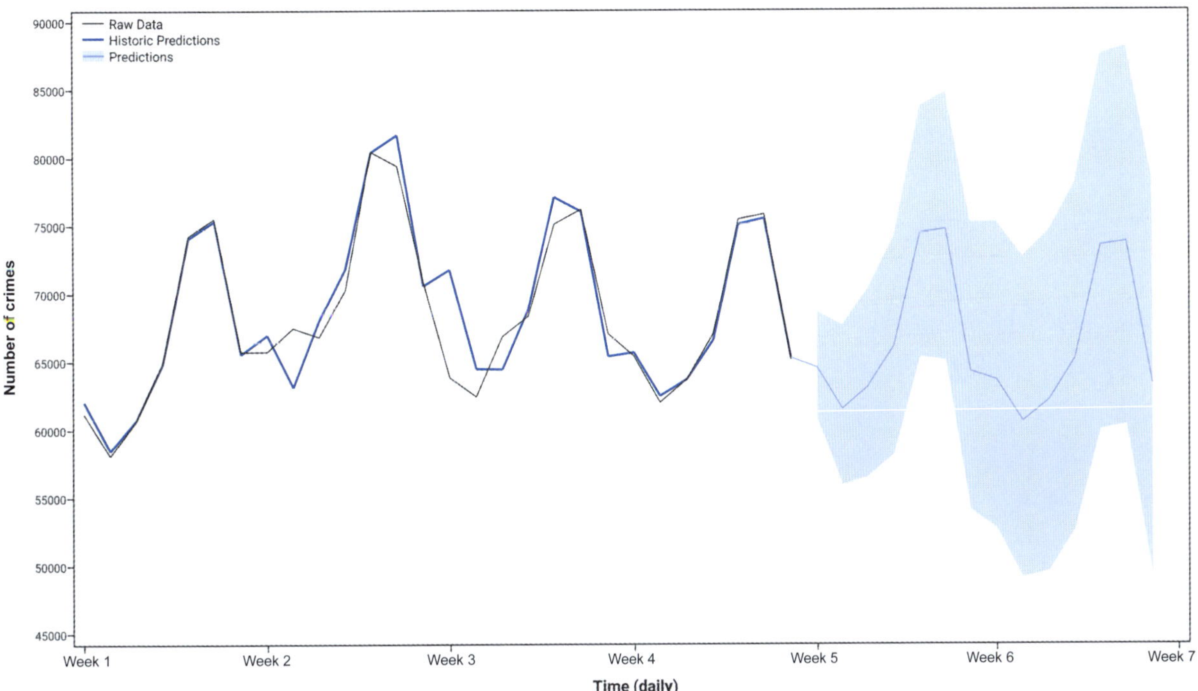

Time	Min	Prediction	Max
Week5D1	60529	64531	68738
Week5D2	55786	61500	66828
Week5D3	55763	63067	69585
Week5D4	57875	66083	73215
Week5D5	65908	74417	82896
Week5D6	64689	74690	84285
Week5D7	53655	64247	74200
Week6D1	52277	63613	74801
Week6D2	48076	60582	72644
Week6D3	49821	62150	75308
Week6D4	52581	65165	78622
Week6D5	59955	73500	87477
Week6D6	60522	73773	88556
Week6D7	49527	63329	78550

ISBN: 9780170472975

4 Forecasts for the average number of pneumococcal cases per month in New Zealand.

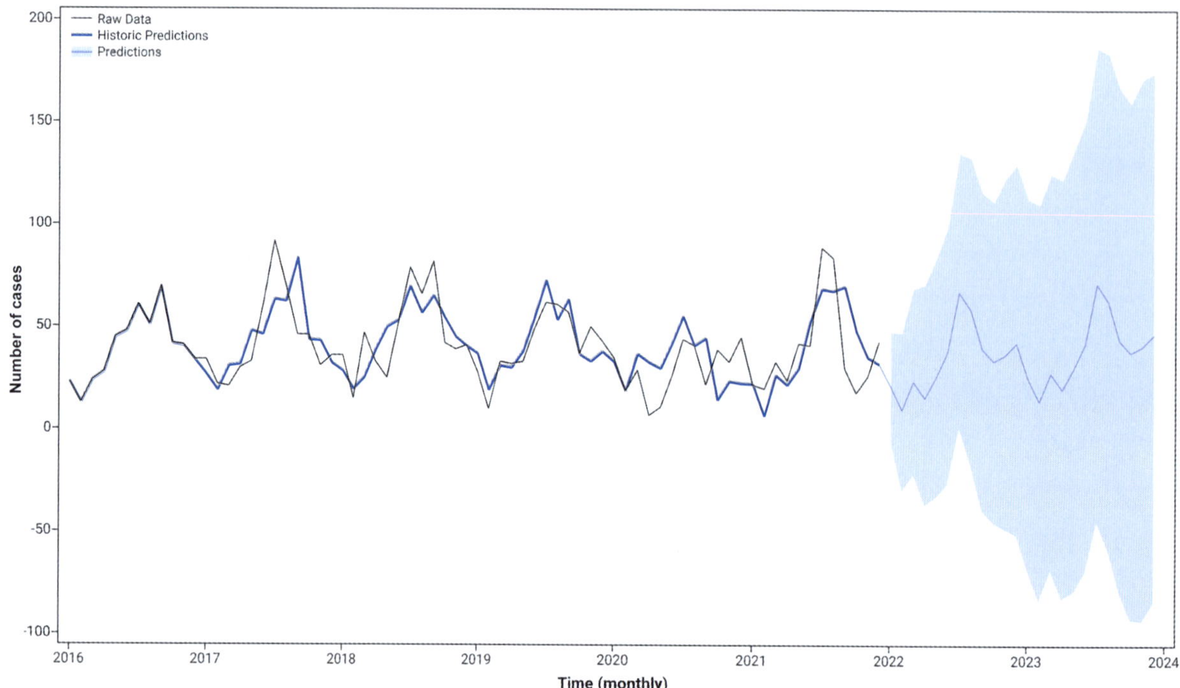

Time	Min	Prediction	Max
2022M01	–4.5045	21.85	47.698
2022M02	–30.414	10.471	47.612
2022M03	–20.899	24.247	72.965
2022M04	–38.751	16.297	70.35
2022M05	–33.486	26.669	86.973
2022M06	–28.069	38.756	10158
2022M07	–1.8024	68.048	136.2
2022M08	–13.908	59.571	133.77
2022M09	–36.115	40.337	119.4
2022M10	–45.769	34.269	117.59
2022M11	–49.176	37.3	129.91
2022M12	–48.639	43.077	137.23
2023M01	–72.95	26.016	120.35
2023M02	–83.882	14.637	119.91
2023M03	–77.228	28.413	132.71
2023M04	–85.85	20.463	123.08
2023M05	–77.408	30835	139.43
2023M06	–67.34	42.922	150.3
2023M07	–38.386	72.214	188.59
2023M08	–54.495	63.737	178.66
2023M09	–75.368	44.503	167.19
2023M10	–81.457	38.435	161.84
2023M11	–79.394	41.466	164.81
2023M12	–74.577	47.243	173.02

ISBN: 9780170472975

7 Communicate findings in a conclusion

In your conclusion you should:
- Repeat earlier important points
- Make a judgement about the reliability of the forecasts
- Discuss whether the information you have learnt in your report is useful and who it might it be useful for
- Discuss limitations of the report and how it could be improved
- **Do not** include new information. This is where you should be summing up your ideas.

Putting it all together

The following are the **requirements** for a basic report. These have been numbered in the report on pages 44–45.

1 Research your context.

2 Select a suitable variable that is informed by contextual knowledge.

3 State the purpose of your investigation and who would find it useful.

4 Describe and quantify the trend.

5 Describe and quantify the seasonality.

6 Make a forecast in context.

7 Communicate findings in a conclusion.

Time series basic report — Milk powder exports from New Zealand

I will investigate the amount of milk powder exported from New Zealand. This data set is quarterly from 2013 to the end of 2021. It has been sourced from Statistics New Zealand (http://infoshare.stats.govt.nz/). Milk powder is New Zealand's biggest goods export, which makes it important for the economy. *https://www.stats.govt.nz/news/dairy-exports-to-china-down-in-december.*

1 Research context.
2 Select suitable variable.

Forecasts for this data set could be useful for the government, farmers, and companies like Fonterra.

3 Purpose.

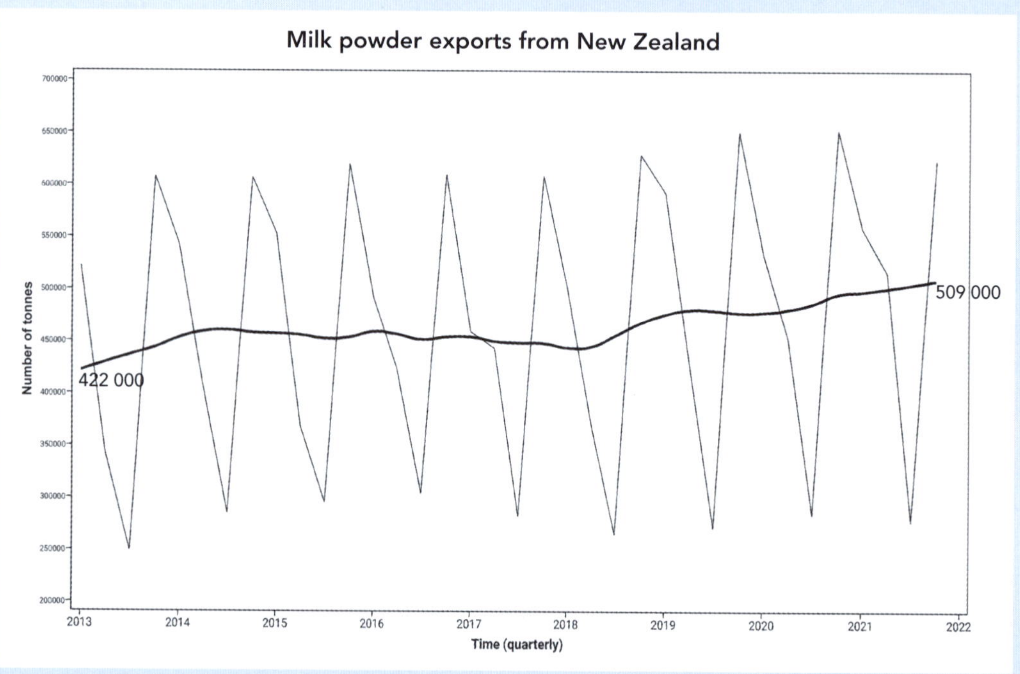

There is an overall increase in the trend for the amount of milk powder exports from New Zealand from 422 000 tonnes per quarter at the start of 2013 to 509 000 tonnes per quarter at the end of 2021.

4 Trend described and quantified.

Milk powder exports increased during 2013, and then were stable through to early 2018. They increased substantially between early 2018 until early 2019. After that, they increased slowly until the end of 2021.

There is a similar seasonal pattern each year. In the first quarter, the milk powder exports are around 74 600 tonnes above the average. In the second quarter, they are around 51 500 tonnes below the average. In the third quarter, they are around 185 800 tonnes below average exported. In the fourth quarter, there are around 162 200 tonnes above the average.

5 Seasonality quantified.

ISBN: 9780170472975

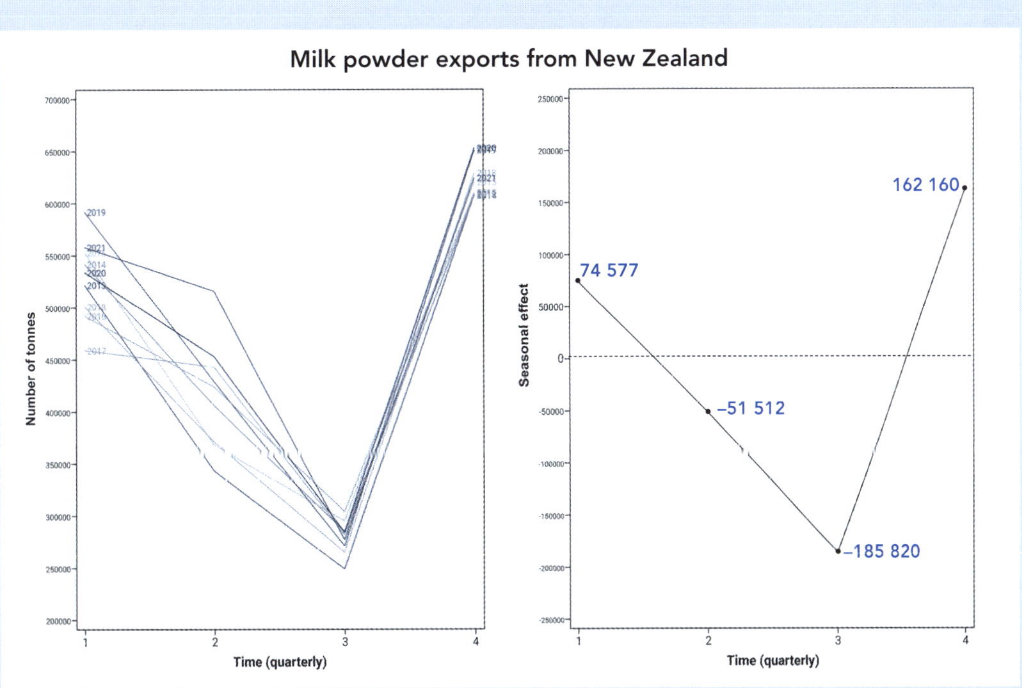

The largest amount of milk powder is exported in the fourth quarter, and the least is in the third quarter. This is likely to have something to do with the milking season.

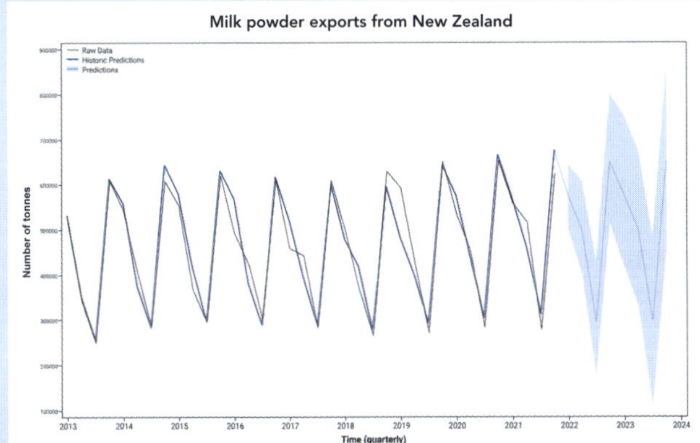

Time	Min	Prediction	Max
2022Q1	506160	574030	643490
2022Q2	401820	497360	597330
2022Q3	171390	293980	423760
2022Q4	511560	648870	792360
2023Q1	418470	675350	739920
2023Q2	323360	499680	676520
2023Q3	112700	296310	484060
2023Q4	459580	651190	847000

We can predict that the amount of milk powder to be exported from New Zealand in the first quarter of 2022 will be approximately 574 000 tonnes. We can be 95% confident that the amount of milk powder exported from New Zealand in Quarter 1 of 2022 will be between 506 200 and 643 500 tonnes. 6 Forecast quantified in context.

In conclusion, there has been an overall increase of about 90 000 tonnes in the amount of milk powder being exported from New Zealand between 2013 and the end of 2021. There is a strong seasonal pattern that has been fairly consistent.

Because both the trend and the seasonal pattern are reasonably consistent, I think the forecasts will be reliable. 7 Conclusion.

ISBN: 9780170472975

Improving your report

A Looking at the data more closely and researching your findings.

- Trend — Average increase/decrease + Reasons
  — Any periods of significant increase or decrease + Reasons.
- Seasonal pattern and identifying unusual seasonal values.
- Recomposition.

B Forecast reliability looking at:

- Seasonal consistency.
- Historical predictions.
- Robustness.

C Comparing, contrasting or combining variables.

D Developing understanding of Holt-Winters model.

E Looking into another model (multiplicative).

F Splitting the data into phases.

Note:

- Not all data sets will be suitable for all of these improvements.
- Incorporate these improvements within your report as you go.
- You may be aware of the reasons, e.g. earthquakes or Covid, but you should still reference a reputable website that confirms your thoughts.
- Sometimes it won't be possible to find reasons for your observations.

ISBN: 9780170472975

A Looking at the data more closely and researching your findings

You can add more detail to your report by looking more closely at:

- Trend
- Seasonal pattern and identifying unusual seasonal values
- Recomposition.

Trend

You can add to this by:

- Calculating the overall increase or decrease
- Looking for periods of significant increase or decrease and researching the reasons for these.

Example:

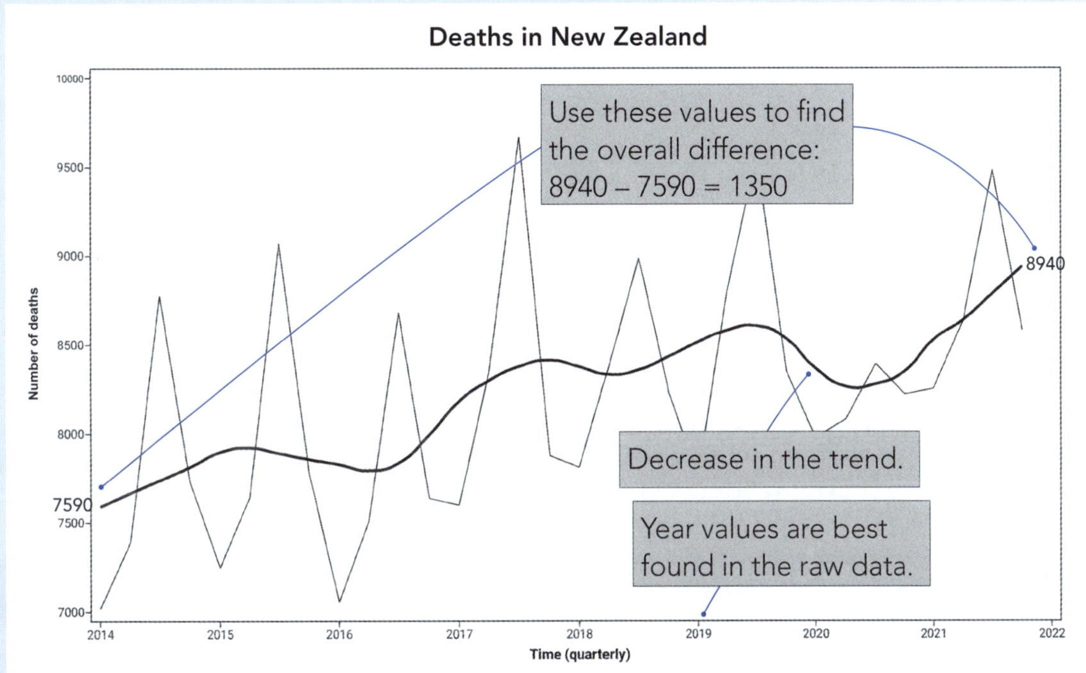

Average increase/decrease

Over the eight years, the average number of quarterly deaths increases by 1350.
∴ The **average** increase in the number of quarterly deaths is 168.75 per **year**.

$$\frac{1350}{8} = 168.75$$

Reason: Further research required, e.g. is this a result of an increasing population?

Periods of significant increase or decrease

There was a notable decrease in the number of deaths in New Zealand in 2020.

Reason: This has been attributed to the reduction of influenza, probably a result of the lockdown due to Covid. https://www.thelancet.com/article/S0140-6736(20)32647-7/fulltext

Calculate the average increase or decrease per year and identify any periods of significant increase or decrease in the trend for these data sets. Where possible, give reasons.

1 The graphs show the amount of sugar and sugar confectionery (tonnes) imported into New Zealand each month from the start of 2014 until the end of 2021.

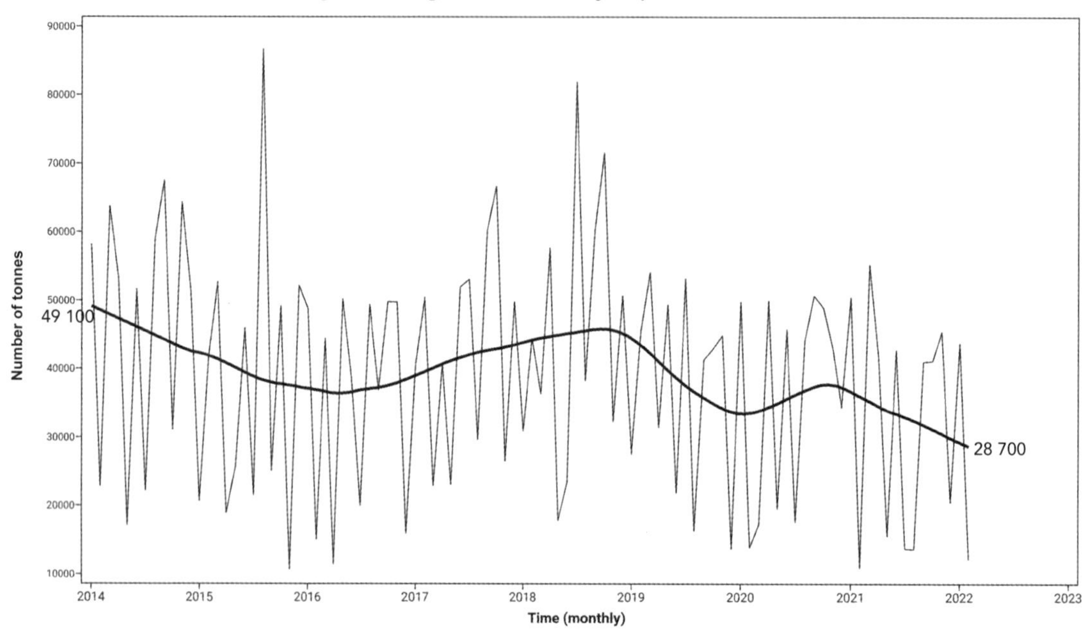

Average increase/decrease

Calculation = $\dfrac{\_\_\_\_\_ - \_\_\_\_\_}{8}$ = ________

There is an **average** increase/decrease in the __________ amount of sugar and sugar confectionery imported into New Zealand of __________ tonnes per __________.

Reasons: ____________________

Periods of significant increase or decrease (if any)

____

Reasons: ____________________

 ISBN: 9780170472975

2 The graph shows the amount of milk powder (tonnes) exported from New Zealand each month from the start of 2013 until the end of 2021.

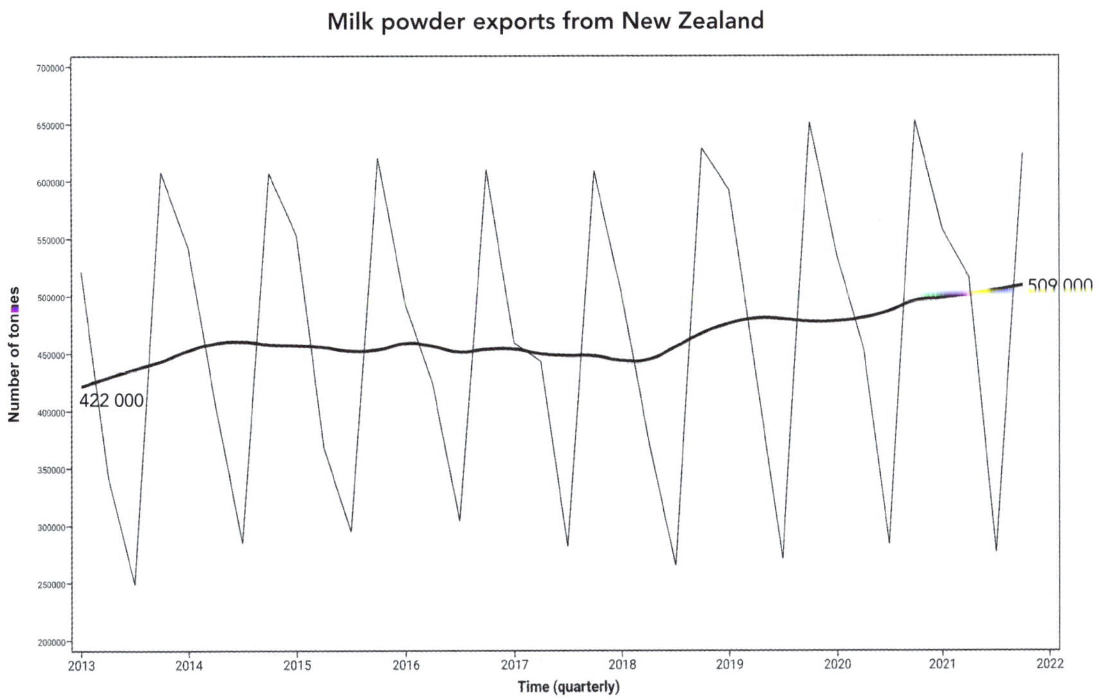

Milk powder exports from New Zealand

Number of tonnes

700000
650000
600000
550000
500000
450000
400000
350000
300000
250000
200000

422 000

509 000

2013 2014 2015 2016 2017 2018 2019 2020 2021 2022

Time (quarterly)

Average increase/decrease

Calculation = $\frac{\_\_\_\_ - \_\_\_\_}{9}$ = ________

There is an **average** increase/decrease in the ____

____.

Reasons: ____

Periods of significant increase or decrease (if any)

____

Reasons: ____

ISBN: 9780170472975

3 The graph shows the number of court proceedings per month for all offences in New Zealand from July 2014 until the end of 2021.

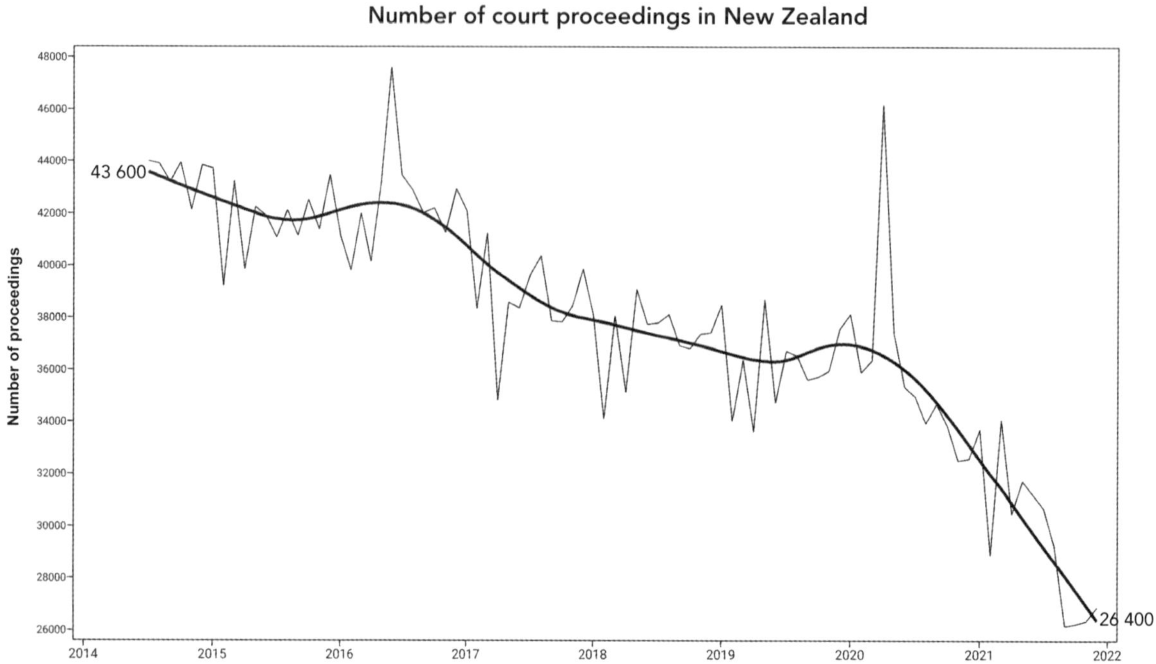

Average increase/decrease

Periods of significant increase or decrease (if any)

ISBN: 9780170472975

4 The graph shows the number of salmonellosis cases in New Zealand per month from the start of 2016 until the end of 2021.

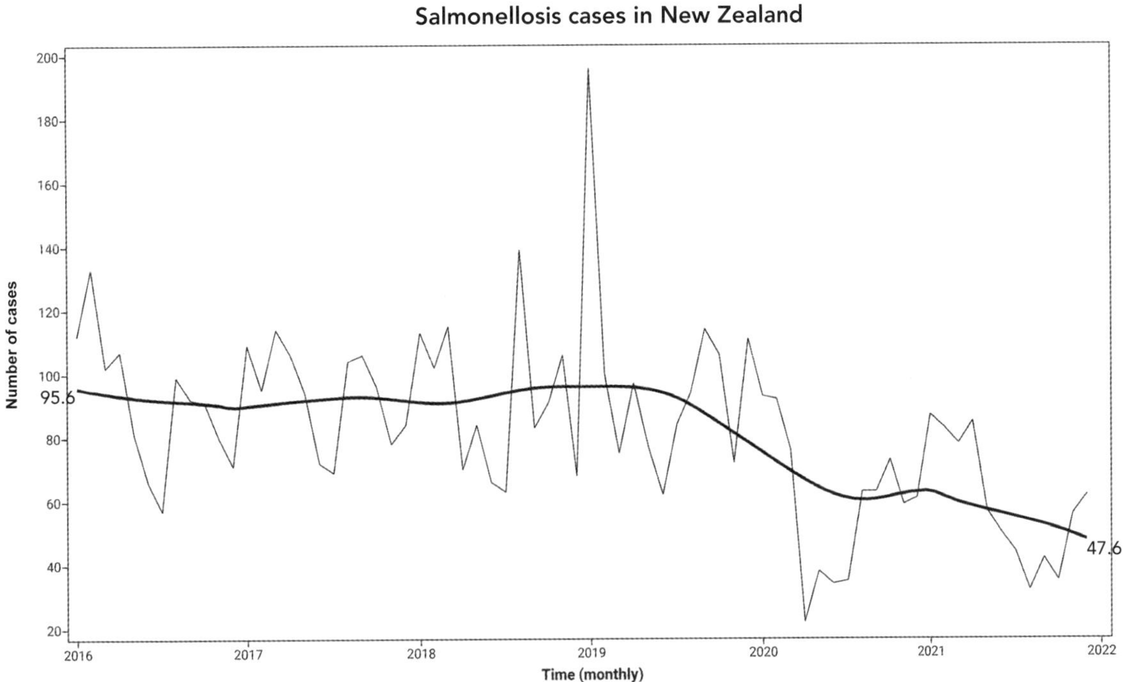

ISBN: 9780170472975

Seasonal pattern and identifying unusual seasonal values

- When graphing the seasonal effects, the 'rainbow' graph cuts the data into years and plots them on top of one another.
- This allows us to recognise whether:
  1 The seasonal pattern is consistent (a similar pattern repeated each year) or inconsistent (the lines are very different).
  2 There are unusual points. Where the pattern is consistent, there may be odd seasons which differ from the rest.

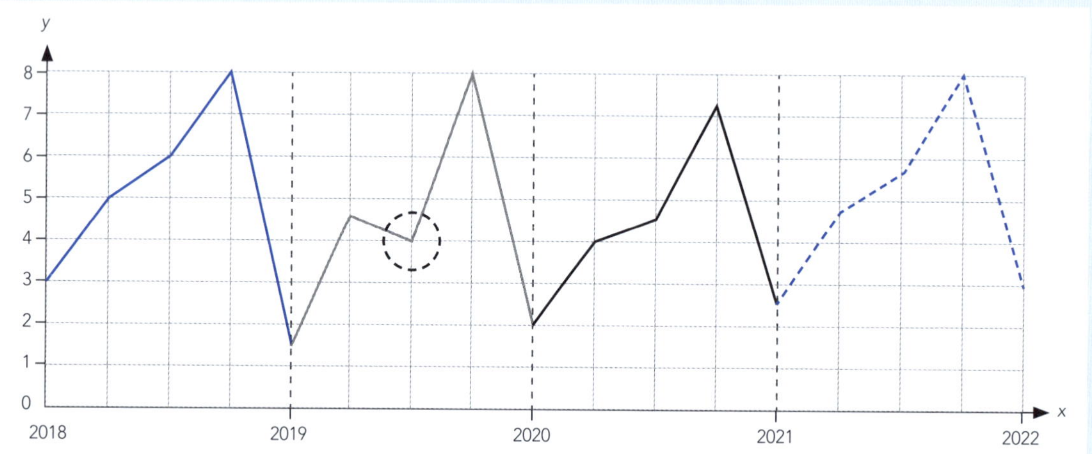

'Cutting' along the vertical dashed lines produces the seasonal data for each of the four years.
These are laid on top of one another.

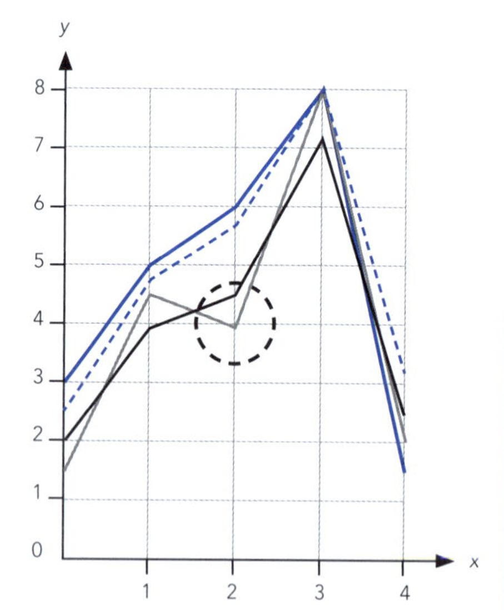

This shows us that:

1 The seasonal pattern is fairly consistent.
2 There is one point which doesn't fit with the pattern. The value for Quarter 2 of 2019 is unexpectedly low. When this occurs, do some research to find the reason.

  ISBN: 9780170472975

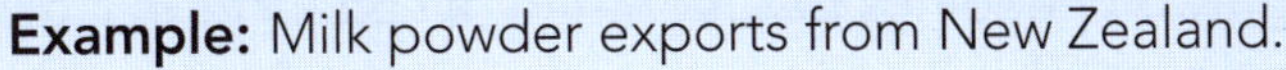

Example: Milk powder exports from New Zealand.

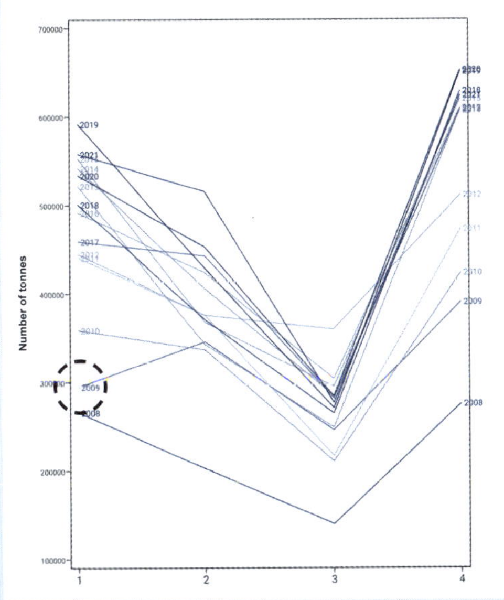

The seasonal pattern is reasonably consistent apart from parts of 2008 and 2009.

In the last three quarters of 2008 and first quarter of 2009, it can be seen that the amount of milk exported was significantly lower than in any other equivalent quarter. This was due to a melamine contamination scare in China.

https://www.rnz.co.nz/news/national/3715/contaminated-milk-scandal-hurting-fonterra

Comment on the consistency of the seasonal pattern. Highlight or circle any unusual features in these graphs and research their causes. You may not always be able to find reasons.

1 The graph shows the number of salmonellosis cases in New Zealand per month from the start of 2016 until the end of 2021.

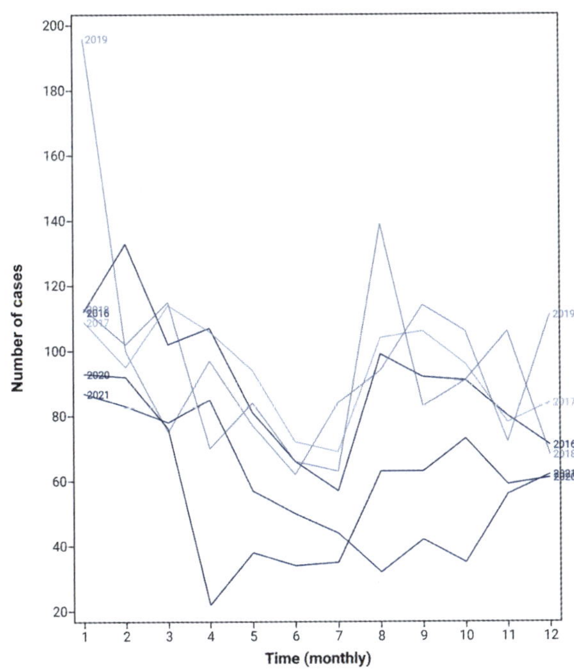

Seasonal pattern: ______________________

____

____

Unusual points and explanations:

____

____

____

____

____

____

____

Hint: January 2019 outbreak: https://www.foodsafetynews.com/2021/06/salmonella-infections-investigated-in-new-zealand/

ISBN: 9780170472975

2 The graph shows the number of court proceedings per month for all offences in New Zealand from July 2018 until the end of 2021.

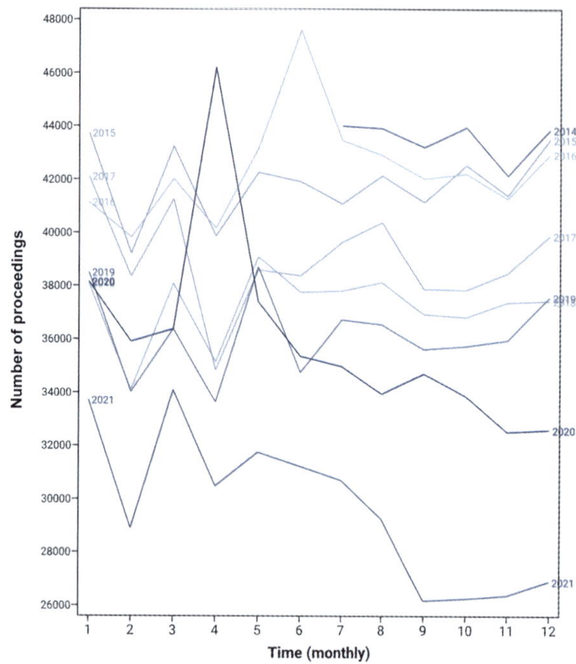

Seasonal pattern:

Unusual points and explanations:

3 The graph shows the number of sheep slaughtered each month in New Zealand from the start of 2018 until the end of 2021.

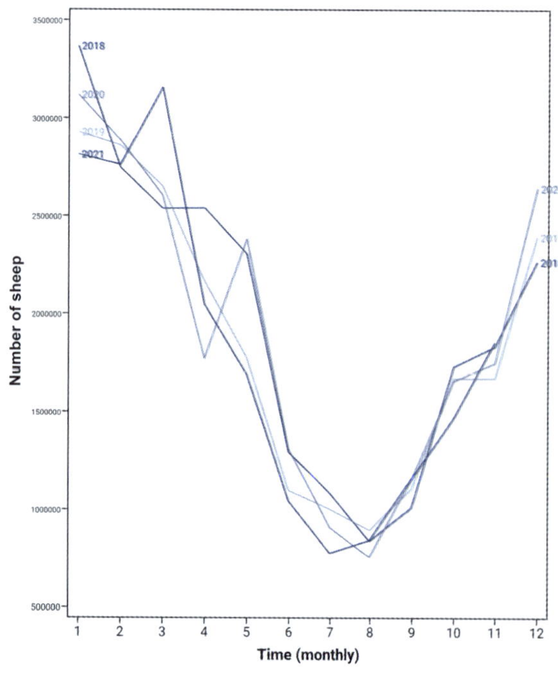

Seasonal pattern:

Unusual points and explanations:

ISBN: 9780170472975

4 The graph shows the number of deaths in New Zealand from the start of 2014 until the end of 2021.

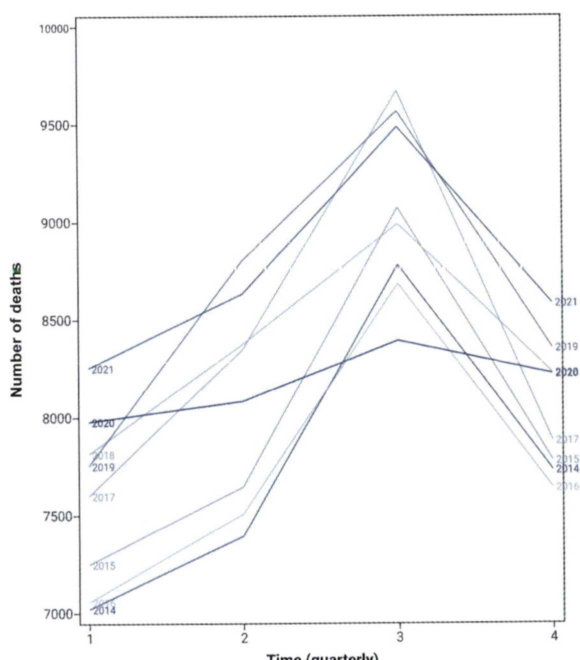

5 The graph shows the number of cases of invasive pneumococcal disease in New Zealand from the start of 2016 until the end of 2021.

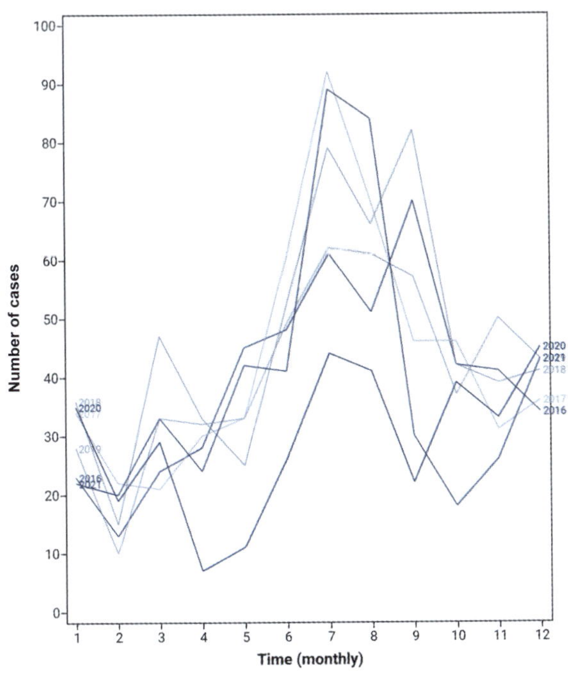

ISBN: 9780170472975

Recomposition

The recomposition graph shows the original data, the trend, the seasonality and the residuals.

- Residuals give you the difference between the data value and the model value.

Residual value = actual data value – model data value

- If a residual is greater than 10% of the total range of the data, the data point is considered to be an **unusual point**.
- Some graphing programs show lines representing the 10% threshold on the residual graph.
- The unusual points that you identify here will probably be the same as those identified when examining the seasonal pattern. However, they are more easily spotted on these recomposition graphs.

This graph shows the recomposed data for deaths in New Zealand between 2014 and 2022.

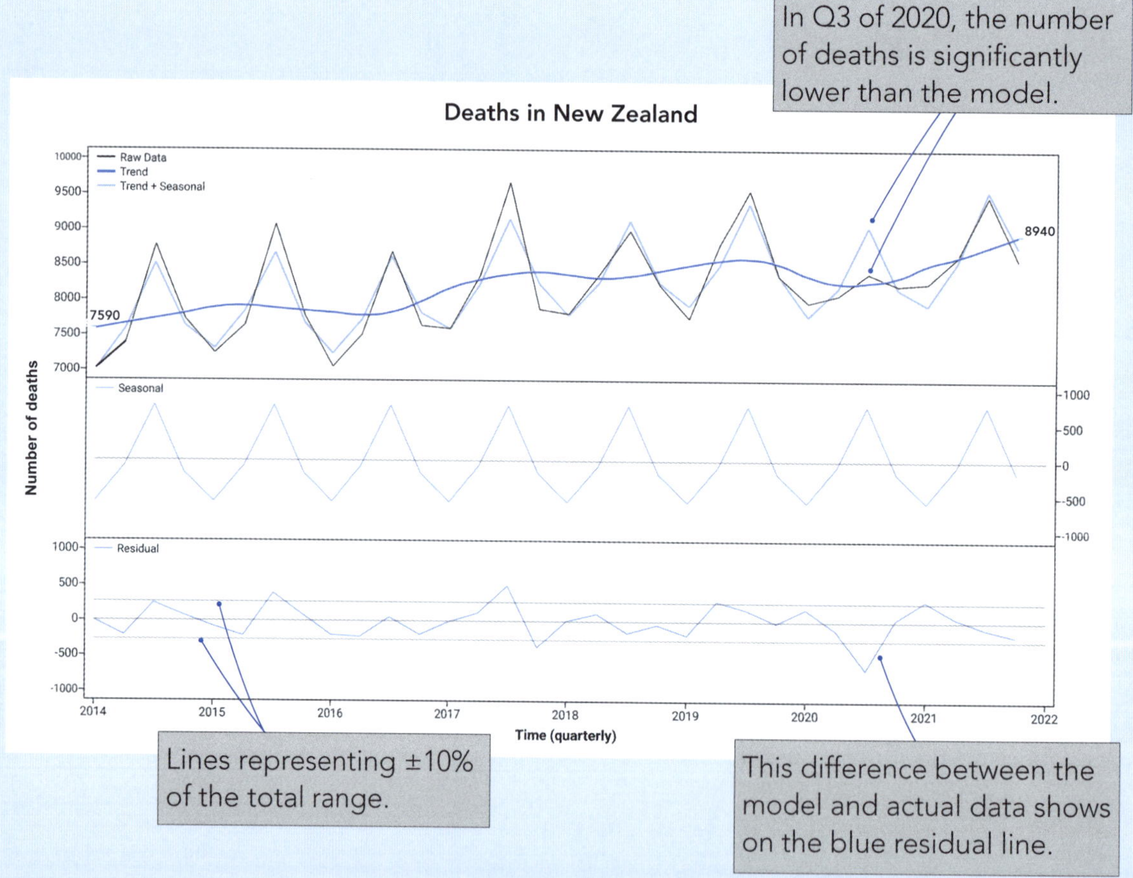

The reduction in the number of deaths in New Zealand in the third quarter of 2020 was attributed to Covid protocols lowering the transmission of communicable diseases that can cause death. https://www.newshub.co.nz/home/new-zealand/2021/05/coronavirus-nz-only-oecd-country-to-have-fewer-deaths-than-expected-in-2020-study.html

As a general rule, any point above or below the 10% residual lines will be worth researching.

ISBN: 9780170472975

Highlight or circle the residuals that are worth investigating for these data sets. You may not always be able to find reasons.

1 This graph shows the number of sheep slaughtered in New Zealand between 2018 and 2022.

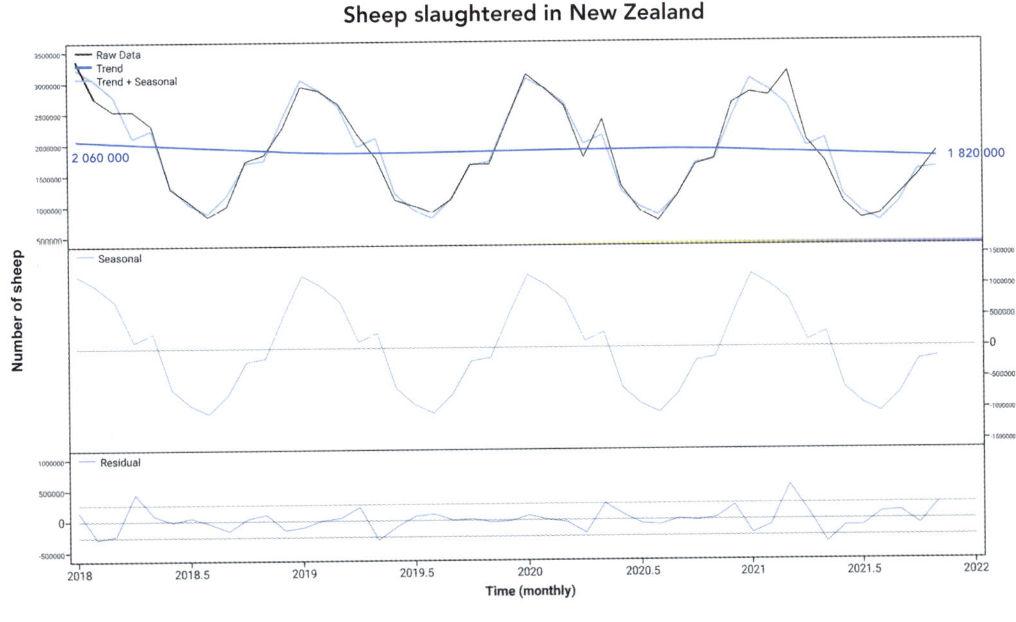

2 The graph shows the number of court proceedings per month for all offences in New Zealand from July 2014 until the end of 2021.

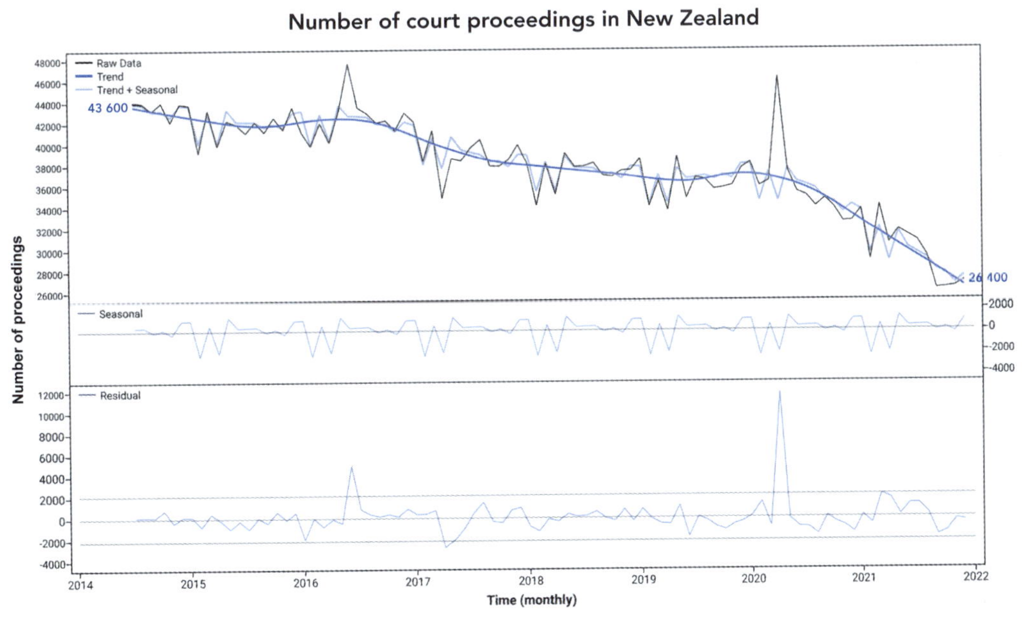

ISBN: 9780170472975

B Forecast reliability

- Ideally a statement should be made about how reliable the forecasts are.
- Three things can help with this:
  - Seasonal consistency
  - Historical predictions
  - Robustness check.

Seasonal consistency

- The graphs below show the individual seasonal effects.
- It can be difficult to read these values, particularly when the lines overlap. Often the graphing program is useful, as you can hover over points to get more information.

Examples:

1 Deaths in New Zealand.

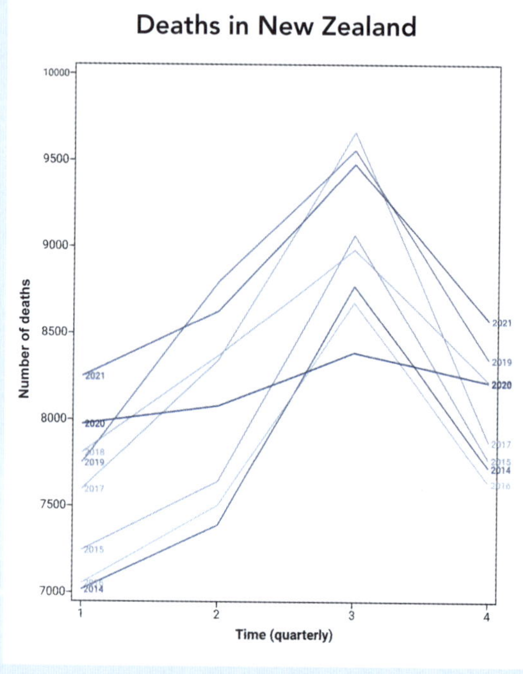

All years show a similar seasonal pattern, with a peak in the third quarter. However, in 2020 it was much less pronounced. The consistent seasonal pattern will increase the reliability of the forecasts.

2 Births in New Zealand.

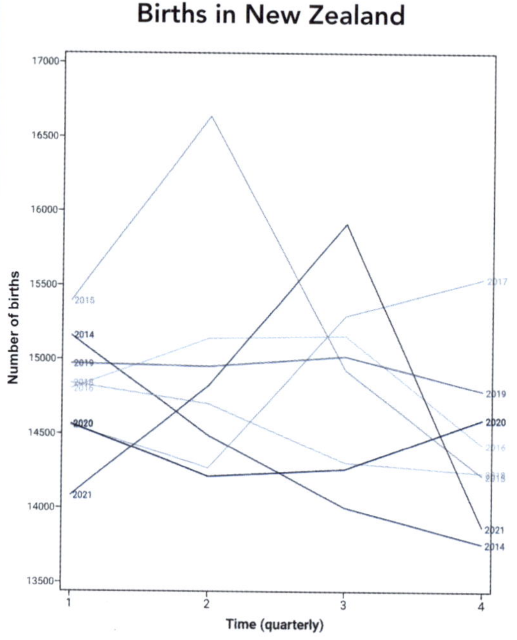

The number of births, however, is much less consistent, and this will make the forecasts less reliable.

 ISBN: 9780170472975

Historical predictions

- The graphs below show the original data and historical predictions.
- If the historical predictions are similar to the actual data, and conditions remain similar, then forecasts are more likely to be reliable.

Examples:

1 The numbers of deaths in New Zealand between 2014 and 2024.

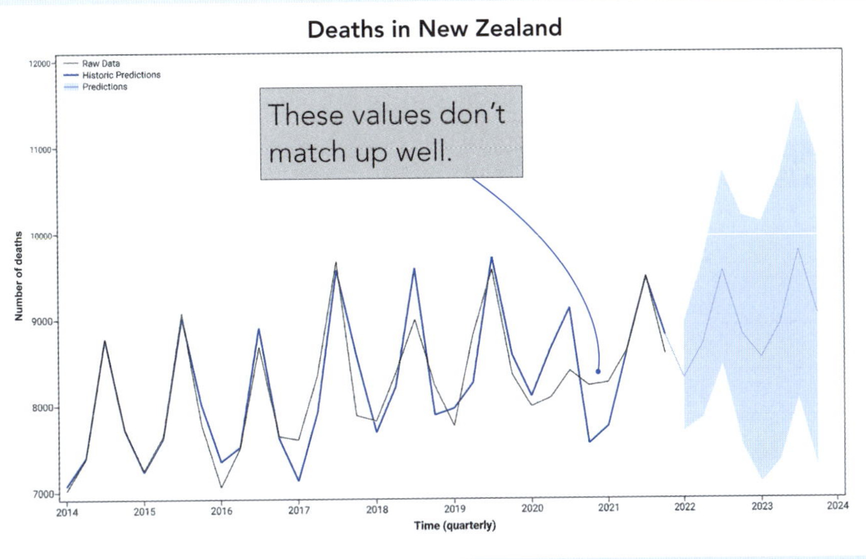

These historic predictions are similar to the actual data, apart from in 2020. These differences will decrease the reliability of the forecasts.

2 The numbers of births in New Zealand between 2014 and 2024.

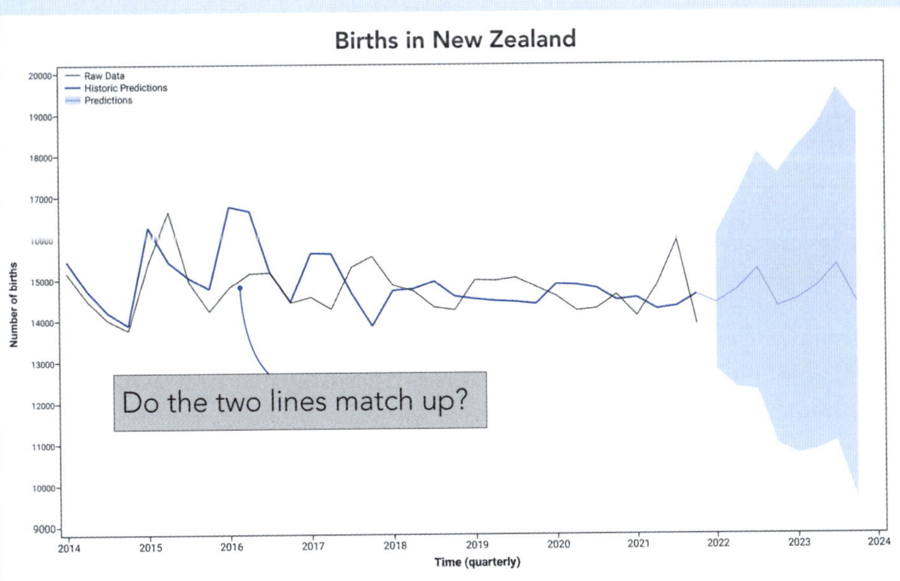

The historic predictions for the numbers of births are not very similar to the actual data. This means that the forecasts are unlikely to be reliable.

ISBN: 9780170472975

Robustness check

- Performing a robustness check is a way of checking whether forecasts are likely to be reliable.

Steps

1. Remove the final 'cycle' (one year's worth) of data.
2. Use previous data to make forecasts for these removed values, including their confidence intervals.
3. Check whether the real values lie within the predicted confidence intervals.

Here is the latest data on the number of deaths in New Zealand.

Time	Total deaths
2020Q1	7977
2020Q2	8082
2020Q3	8391
2020Q4	8220
2021Q1	8244
2021Q2	8619
2021Q3	9522
2021Q4	8580

Remove the last year's worth of data.

Now use your program to make forecasts for 2021.

Time	Min	Prediction	Max
2021Q1	6956	7639.8	8291.3
2021Q2	7185.3	8187.7	9199.8
2021Q3	7845.3	8990.8	10175
2021Q4	6970.1	8267.9	9568.1
2022Q1	6383.5	7798.1	9250.6
2022Q2	67608	8346	10043
2022Q3	740134	9149	10934
2022Q4	6532.3	8426.1	10398

Now check whether the actual values fall within the 95% confidence interval.

Time	Total deaths	
2021Q1	8244	✓
2021Q2	8619	✓
2021Q3	9522	✓
2021Q4	8580	✓

Notice that the predicted numbers of deaths are all lower than the actual numbers.

All four values lie within the confidence intervals. This means that the forecasts are likely to be reliable. However, the prediction for Q1 is only just below the maximum confidence interval.

You could suggest reasons that the model has underestimated the number of deaths in New Zealand for 2021.

Always remember: We are using mathematical models to describe real situations. They will never be perfect.

ISBN: 9780170472975

For each of the following, consider the seasonal pattern, the historic predictions and the robustness check, and from these, decide whether the forecasts are likely to be reliable or not.

1 Numbers of cattle slaughtered in New Zealand.

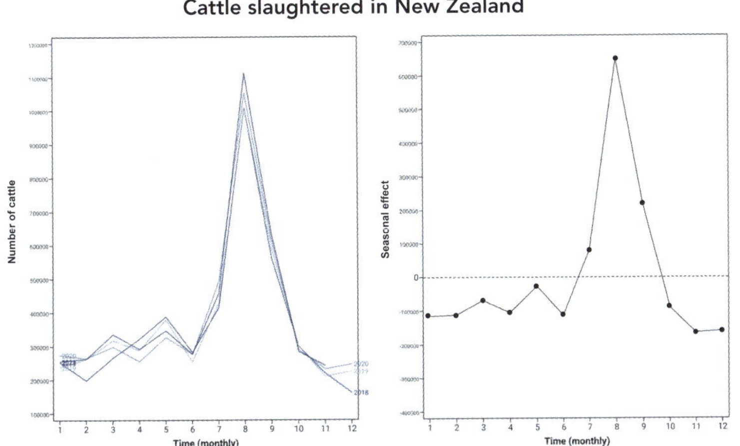

The seasonal pattern is consistent/inconsistent.

This suggests the forecasts are likely to be reliable/unreliable.

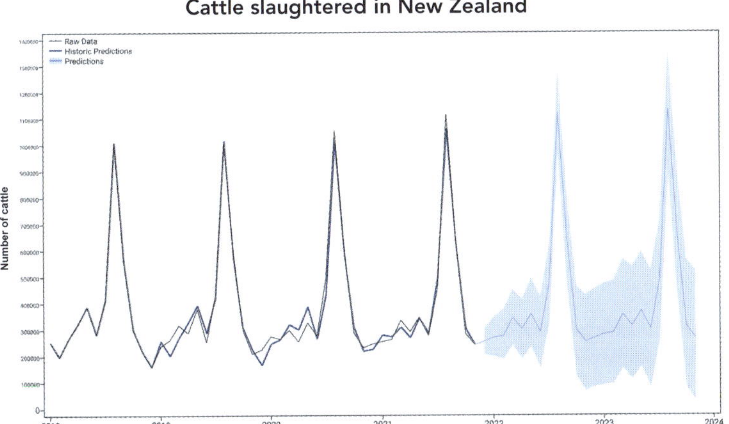

The historic predictions do/do not match up.

This suggests the forecasts are likely to be reliable/unreliable.

Time	Min	Prediction	Max
2021M01	229890	281270	333950
2021M02	196800	271790	344000
2021M03	218380	306340	393810
2021M04	157260	263460	365600
2021M05	223230	335860	452490
2021M06	160010	285810	410970
2021M07	363550	500140	637220
2021M08	912530	1061900	1209400
2021M09	457650	622560	781990
2021M10	122360	298280	462950
2021M11	56720	240510	424160
2021M12	65213	255310	438110

Complete the robustness check.

Time	Total all cattle	
2021M01	255498	✓
2021M02	262905	
2021M03	335427	
2021M04	291931	
2021M05	346708	
2021M06	277093	
2021M07	457222	
2021M08	1113198	
2021M09	631445	
2021M10	284143	
2021M11	241782	
2021M12	232875	

The robustness check suggests the forecasts are likely to be reliable/unreliable.

Overall, these forecasts are likely to be reliable/unreliable.

ISBN: 9780170472975

2 Numbers of pigs slaughtered in New Zealand.

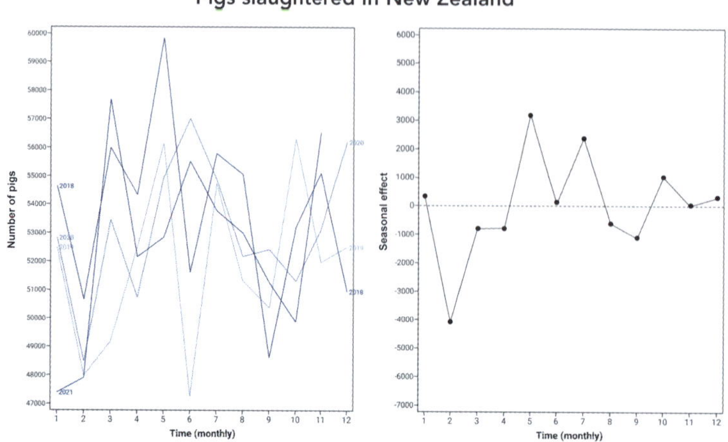

The seasonal pattern is consistent/inconsistent.

This suggests the forecasts are likely to be reliable/unreliable.

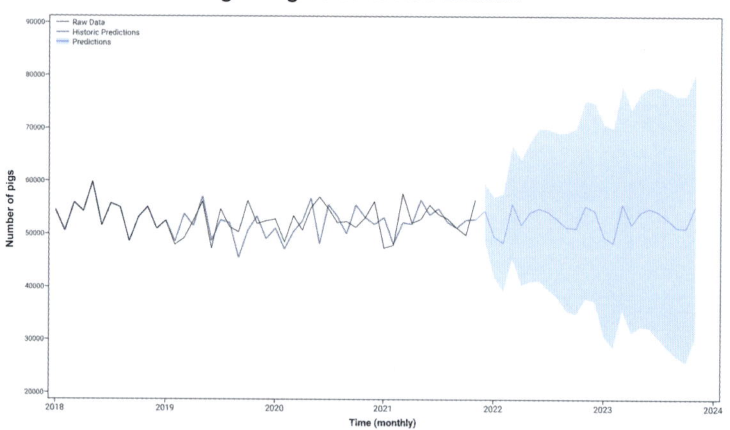

The historic predictions do/do not match up.

This suggests the forecasts are likely to be reliable/unreliable.

Time	Min	Prediction	Max
2021M01	49116	53926	58618
2021M02	43130	50054	56938
2021M03	46032	54913	63234
2021M04	44530	54257	64348
2021M05	48379	59536	70947
2021M06	42477	53855	65767
2021M07	44119	57352	70584
2021M08	41253	56011	69348
2021M09	37305	52337	66228
2021M10	40230	56001	70643
2021M11	40496	57082	73405
2021M12	37604	55662	72134

Time	Total all pigs	
2021M01	47394	✗
2021M02	47904	
2021M03	57685	
2021M04	52151	
2021M05	52835	
2021M06	55518	
2021M07	53778	
2021M08	52994	
2021M09	51261	
2021M10	49870	
2021M11	56538	
2021M12	55600	

Complete the robustness check.

The robustness check suggests the forecasts are likely to be reliable/unreliable.

Overall, these forecasts are likely to be reliable/unreliable.

ISBN: 9780170472975

C Comparing variables

- It is often useful to plot several time series on one graph in order to compare them.
- It can also be useful to compare their seasonal patterns.

Examples:

1 Deaths of males and females in New Zealand.

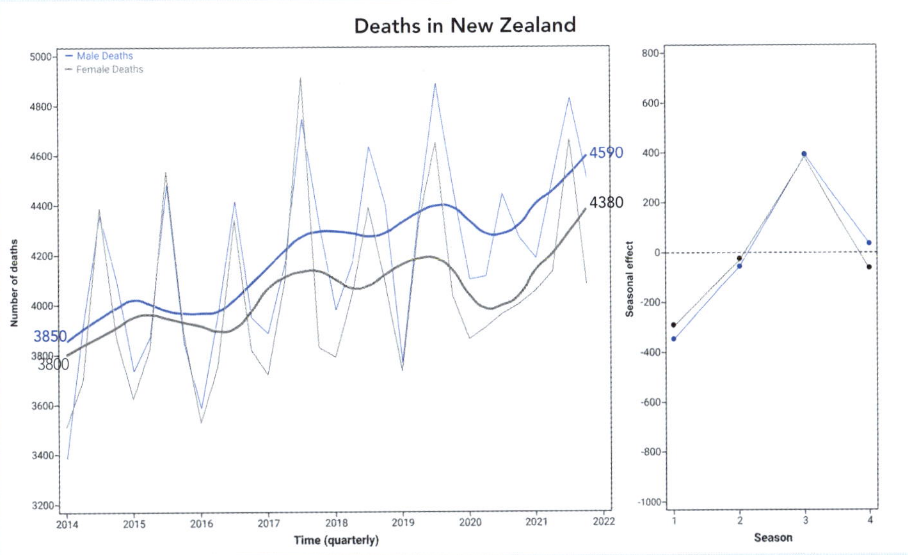

Male and female deaths in New Zealand show similar trends and seasonal patterns. However, there are more males dying than females. A next step could be to look into the numbers of males and females in the population.

2 Numbers of cases of campylobacteriosis and salmonellosis in New Zealand.

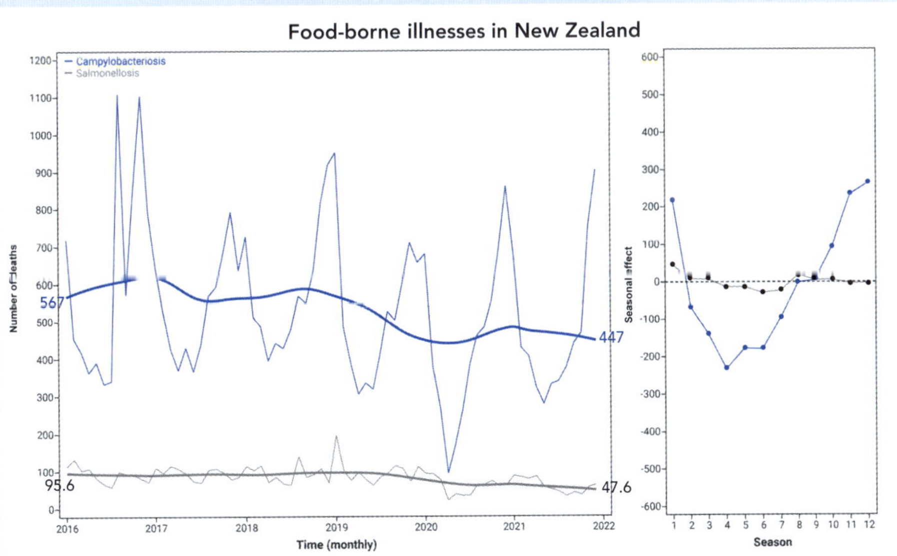

Campylobacteriosis and salmonellosis have significantly different seasonal patterns. There is almost no seasonal effect for salmonellosis, whereas campylobacteriosis is much more common during summer and less in winter. There are also more cases of campylobacteriosis reported than salmonellosis in New Zealand.

ISBN: 9780170472975

What conclusion can you come to when you compare the following sets of data?

1 Total numbers of births and deaths in New Zealand.

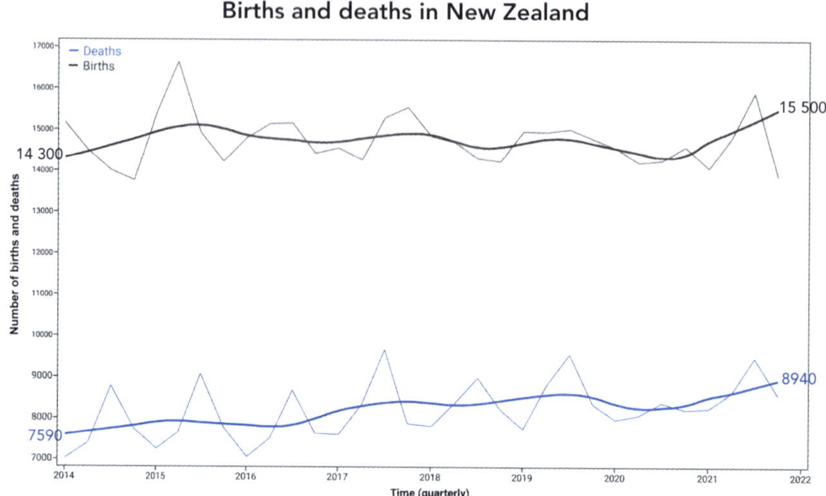

What conclusion could you come to from comparing births and deaths in New Zealand?

What further investigations could this data lead to?

2 The total numbers of sheep and cattle slaughtered in New Zealand.

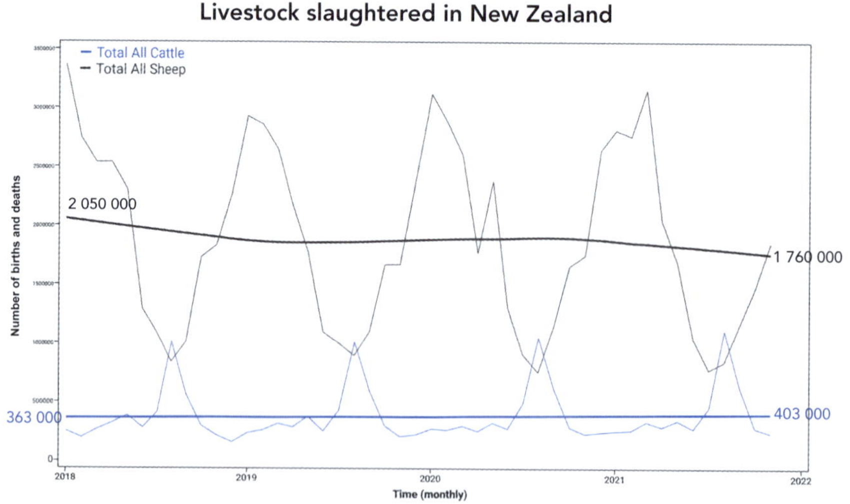

What conclusion could you come to from comparing the numbers of cattle and sheep slaughtered in New Zealand?

What further investigations could this data lead to?

ISBN: 9780170472975

D Developing understanding of Holt-Winters model

Programs for making predictions from time series data use different mathematical models. NZGrapher uses the Holt-Winters model. It's important to understand several aspects of this in order to be able to write with confidence.

Exponential smoothing

- This means that heavier weighting is given to the most recent data values, so they have the greatest impact on the predictions.
- That is why when looking at the trend, it is important to look at the most recent data.

Confidence intervals

- You will have noticed that the confidence interval gets wider the further into the future the forecasts are.
- It is important to be aware that we are still just as confident (95%) regarding these wider intervals. However, the program has given a wider range of values in which the forecast could fall.
- Don't be concerned that the forecasts change each time you get the program to calculate them.

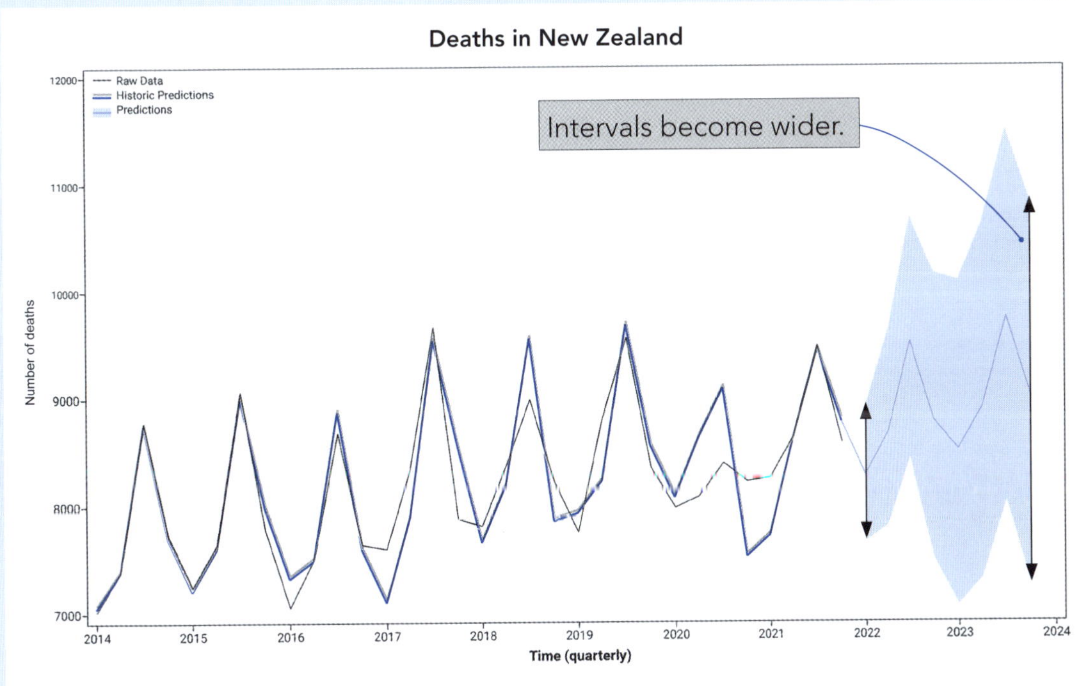

Always remember: We are using mathematical models to describe real situations. They will never be perfect.

ISBN: 9780170472975

An example of where the Holt-Winters model does not work well:

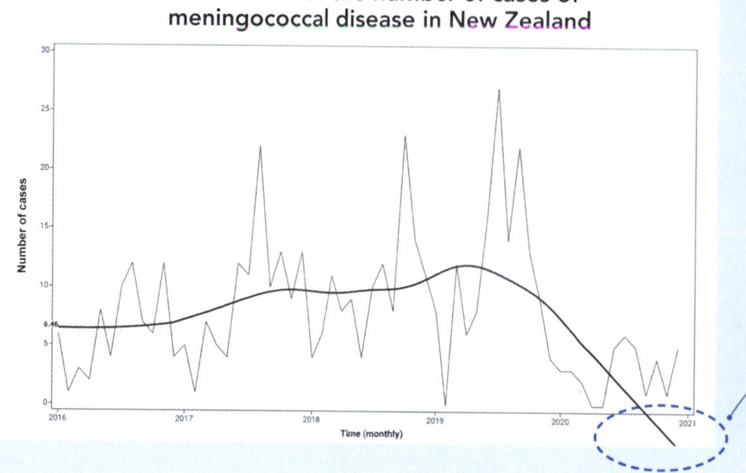

Notice that because of the peaks in cases about the middle of 2019, and the low values in 2020, the trend drops below 0.

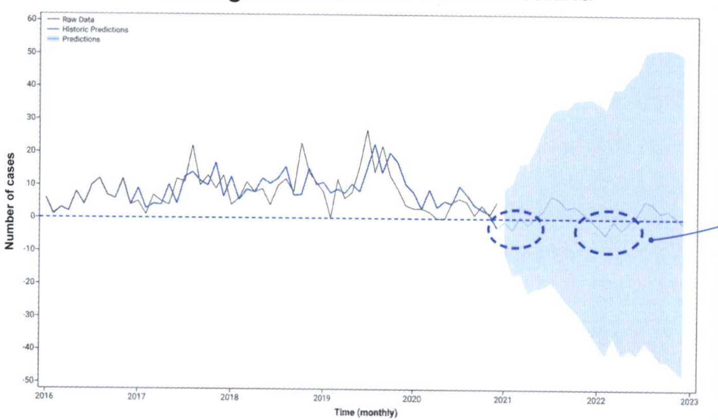

The Holt-Winters model weights the very low numbers of cases in 2020 more heavily than earlier cases. As a result, its predictions are low, and at times it has predicted negative numbers of cases.

Time	Min	Prediction	Max
2021M01	–10.323	–0.80634	9.139
2021M02	–17.036	–3.3207	11.451
2021M03	–15.248	0.82405	17.387
2021M04	–21.021	–1.8451	18.45
2021M05	–21.619	0.55812	22.512
2021M06	–22.81	2.734	26.744
2021M07	–20.478	7.0066	33.33
2021M08	–22.095	5.966	35.287
2021M09	–27.489	3.3387	32.987
2021M10	–28.735	4.0406	35.049
2021M11	–31.866	2.1109	35.597
2021M12	–35.446	0.12686	34.834
2022M01	–38.026	–2.1732	34.601
2022M02	–42.278	–4.6876	32.532
2022M03	–39.431	–0.54282	38.688
2022M04	–41.931	–3.213	36.356
2022M05	–39.863	–0.81375	40.788
2022M06	–40.36	1.3671	43.838
2022M07	–39.16	5.6397	48.679
2022M08	–41.796	4.5991	48.438
2022M09	–43.604	1.9718	47.804
2022M10	–43.115	26.737	48.16
2022M11	–47.316	0.74399	49.648
2022M12	–49.519	–1.24	49.617

If you get negative values in the table, think about whether these are possible. If not, round to 0.

These two groups of negative forecasts are the same as those on the forecast graph.

ISBN: 9780170472975

E Looking into another model (multiplicative)

- For most time series data that you will meet, an **additive** model is appropriate:
  Data value = trend **+** seasonal effect **+** residuals
- Occasionally, a **multiplicative** model is more appropriate:
  Data value = trend **x** seasonal effect **x** residuals

Example:

The graphs show the total number of passenger movements in and out of New Zealand from Q3 of 1978 until Q4 of 2016.

Additive model

There are four aspects of additive time series graphs, which may suggest that a multiplicative model may be more appropriate:

1 Raw data: the amplitude of the seasonal pattern gets bigger or smaller over the data range.

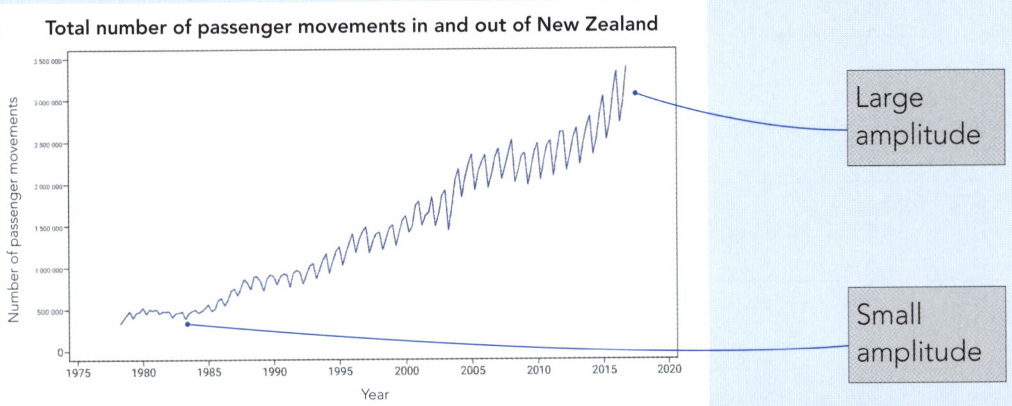

2 Individual seasonal effects: there is a difference in amplitude between start and finish.

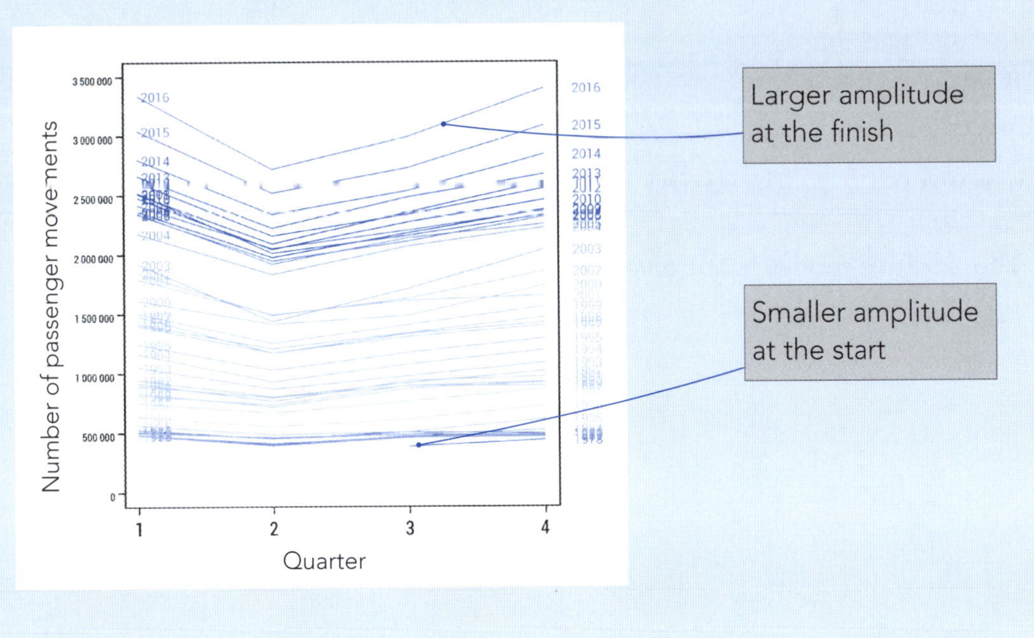

ISBN: 9780170472975

3 Model: does not fit very well, particularly at the start and the finish.

4 Residuals: are bigger at the start and the finish, but small in the middle of the data range.

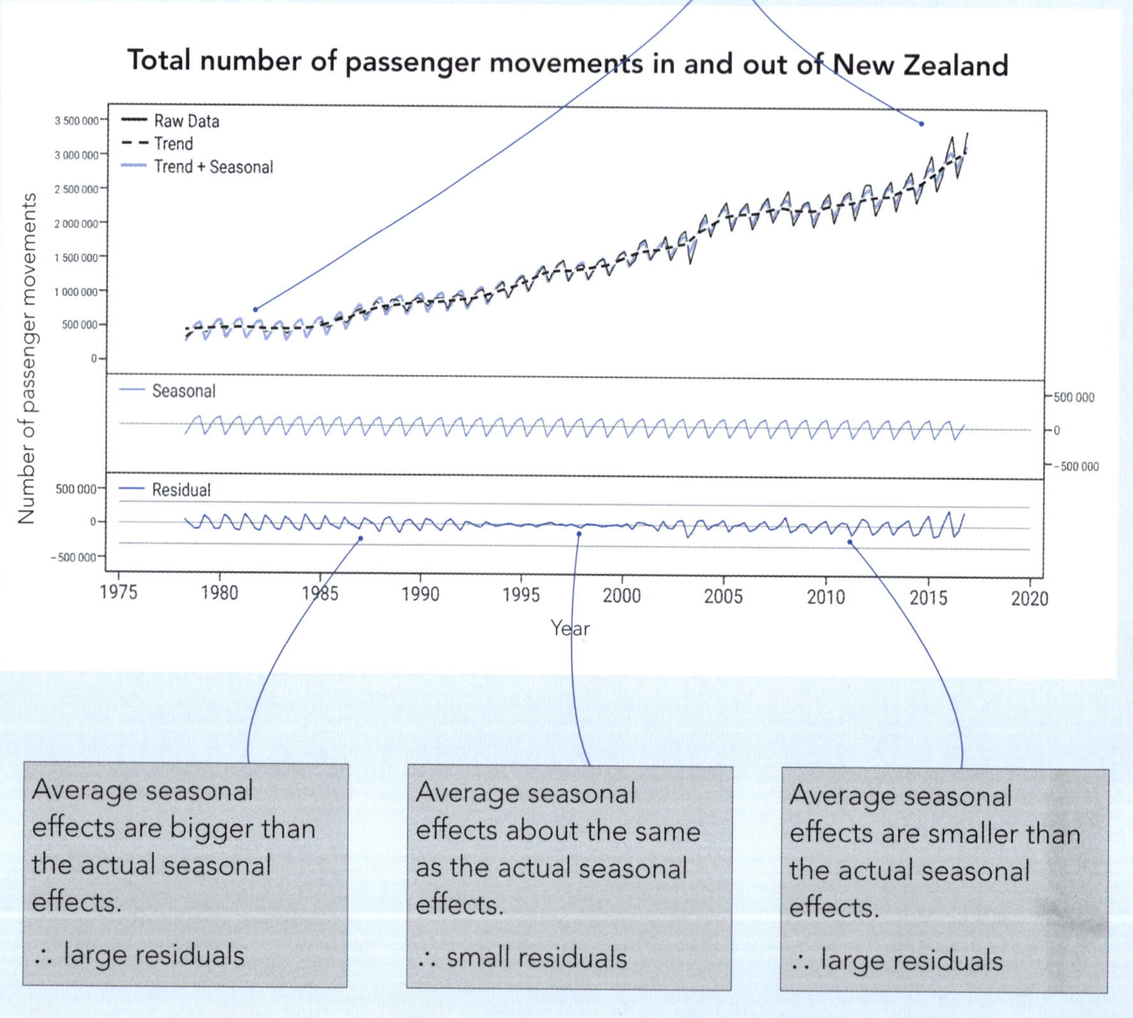

Average seasonal effects are bigger than the actual seasonal effects.

∴ large residuals

Average seasonal effects about the same as the actual seasonal effects.

∴ small residuals

Average seasonal effects are smaller than the actual seasonal effects.

∴ large residuals

∴ **The additive model is not a very good fit for the data.**

ISBN: 9780170472975

Multiplicative model

Notice that the model is a much better fit for the data.

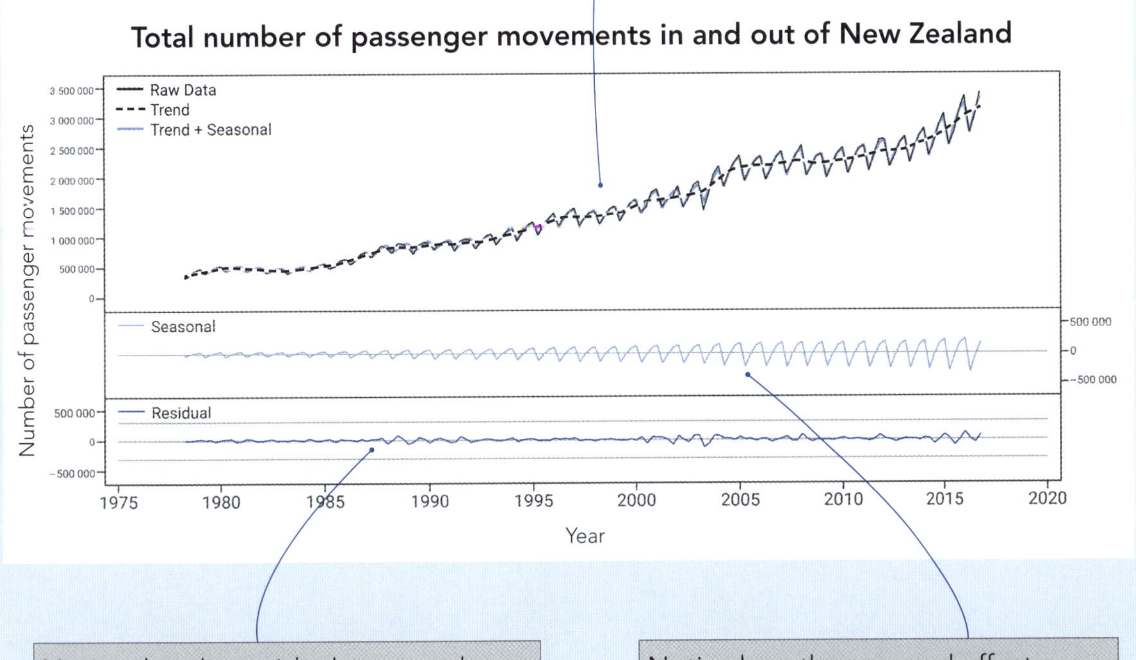

Notice that the residuals are much smaller and without the pattern.

Notice how the seasonal effects increase throughout the series.

A robustness check:

Additive model

Time	Lower 95% boundary	Actual value	Upper 95% boundary	Value within limits?
2016 Q1	3 060 000	3 339 661	3 254 800	✗
2016 Q2	2 489 800	2 719 307	2 777 000	✓
2016 Q3	2 681 600	2 991 162	3 018 100	✓
2016 Q4	2 943 100	3 397 608	3 348 900	✗

Multiplicative model

Time	Lower 95% boundary	Actual value	Upper 95% boundary	Value within limits?
2016 Q1	2 946 400	3 339 661	3 492 300	✓
2016 Q2	2 359 500	2 719 307	2 982 300	✓
2016 Q3	2 485 300	2 991 162	3 328 900	✓
2016 Q4	2 704 900	3 397 608	3 788 100	✓

∴ **The multiplicative model gives more accurate predictions than the additive model.**

ISBN: 9780170472975

F Splitting the data into phases

- Sometimes, usually due to a change of circumstances, there are distinct phases within a time series.
- When these occur, the data should be analysed in sections.
- The purpose of splitting the data is to produce a better model in order to make more reliable predictions.

Example: The graphs show the total number of guest nights in hotels and motels in Canterbury, between the start of 2004 and Q3 of 2016.

Notice that the model does not fit the data very well.

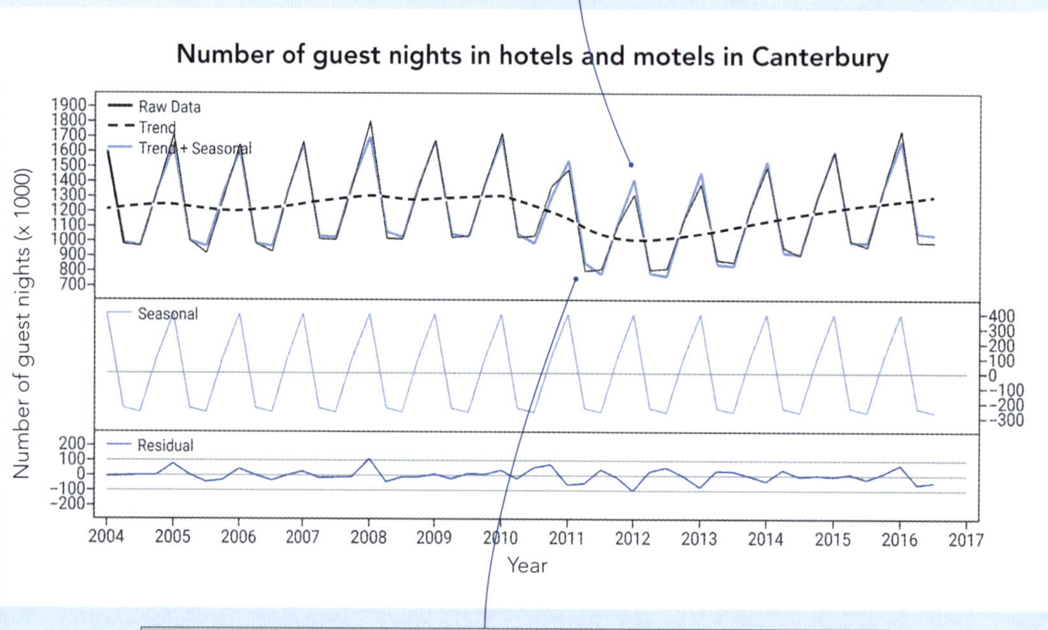

Notice that there was a major change in late 2010 and early 2011 when the Canterbury earthquakes occurred.

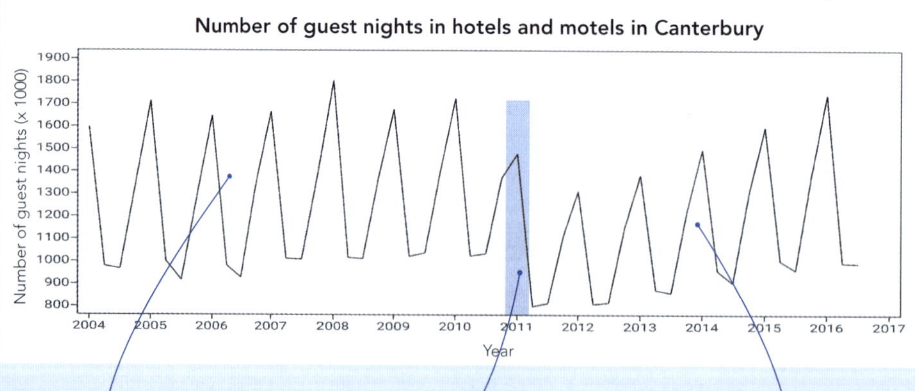

Pre-earthquakes:
Stationary trend.
Seasonal pattern amplitude consistent at about 750 nights.

Period covering most of the earthquakes in 2010/2011.

Post-earthquakes:
Increasing trend.
Seasonal pattern amplitude increasing from about 450 to about 750 nights.

ISBN: 9780170472975

Pre-earthquake phase: due to lack of consistent change in the seasonal pattern, this is best analysed using an additive model.

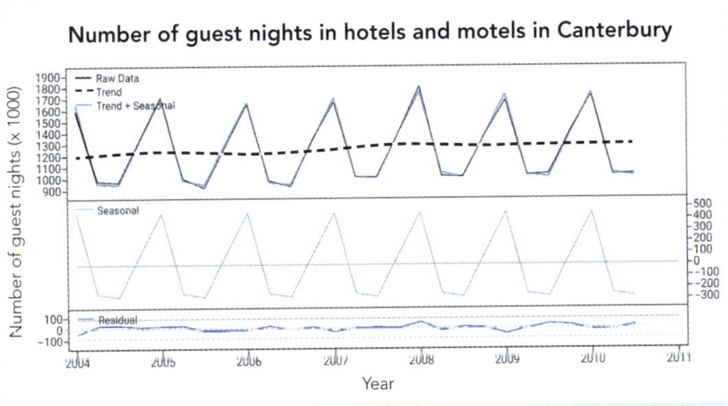

Post-earthquake phase: using an **additive** model.

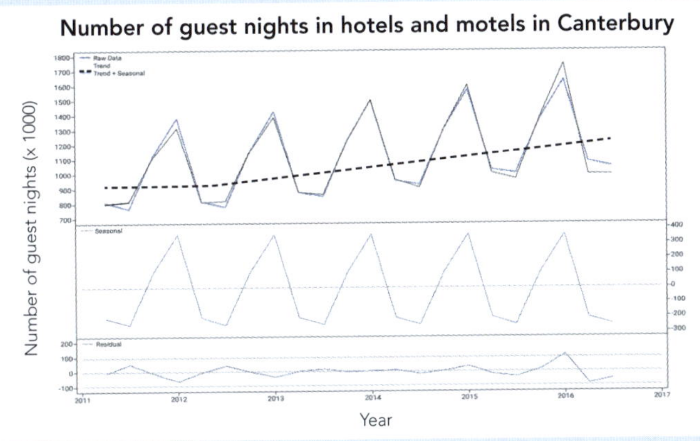

Post-earthquake phase: due to the increasing seasonal pattern, this may be better analysed using a **multiplicative** model.

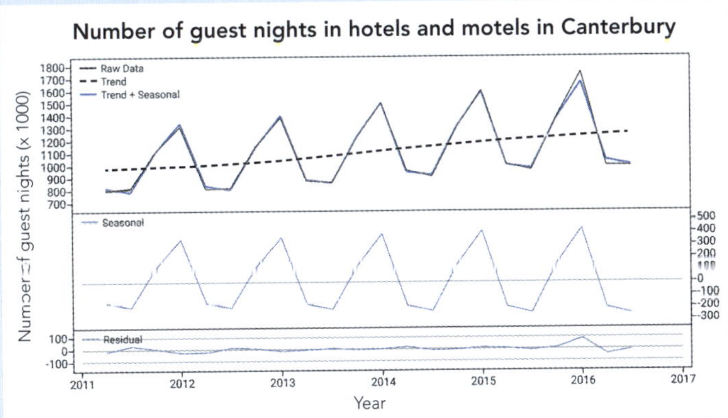

You could then:

1 Make predictions using :
   - The additive model on all the data.
   - The additive model on the data from 2011 to 2016.
   - The multiplicative model on the data from 2011 to 2016.
2 Compare the predictions and use robustness checks.
3 Compare the seasonal pattern for:
   - The additive model for the 2004 to 2010 data.
   - The additive model for the 2011 to 2016 data.

Writing about time series data

When writing about time series data there are very few situations in which you can be definite about what you are stating. Here are some where you can.

Examples:

1 ✗ There **tends to be** an overall increasing trend.
✓ There **is** an overall increasing trend.

2 ✗ The predicted value for the first quarter of 2021 **is about** \$14 980.
✓ The predicted value for the first quarter of 2021 **is** \$14 980.

In nearly all situations you should avoid definite statements.

Examples:

1 ✗ From the graph I can see the average seasonal effect for the first quarter of the year **is** \$218 above the trend.
✓ From the graph I can see the average seasonal effect for the first quarter of the year **is about** \$218 above the trend.

2 ✗ The trend increases by \$480 000 over eight years, which means that **it has increased by** \$60 000 each year.
✓ The trend increases by \$480 000 over eight years, which means that **it has increased on average by** \$60 000 each year.

You should also be careful to match the strength of your statements to the situation.

Examples:

1 ✗ Because the model fits the data closely, we **know** that the forecasts **will be** reliable.
✓ Because the model fits the data closely, we **can have confidence** that the forecasts **will be reasonably** reliable.

2 ✗ Overall there has been a **large** decrease in the trend, about 30% over the 13-year period.
✓ Overall there has been a **moderate** decrease in the trend, about 30% over the 13-year period. (30% over 13 years is only about 2.3% per year.)

ISBN: 9780170472975

Select which is the best from each pair of **blue** terms or phrases..

1 The trend shows that the number of deaths in New Zealand is increasing. However, in 2020 there is a decrease in the trend line. This **is likely to have been/was** due to the reduction in the number of influenza cases due to the Covid restrictions.

2 We can see from the graph that the imports of sugar have been decreasing and **will/are likely to** continue to decrease.

3 The seasonal graph shows **the same/a similar** pattern each year.

4 The 95% confidence limits for the forecasts for the quarterly number of deaths in New Zealand during Q1 of 2022 are 7497 and 8831. This means that the actual number of deaths **will/ is very likely to** lie between these numbers.

5 During the summer months in New Zealand there are fewer deaths because people **don't/are less likely to** contract life-threatening illnesses.

6 There are several significant large residuals, which **means/suggests** that if this model is used to make predictions, they **may/will** not be accurate.

7 The model fits well, so forecasts for the next two years **will be/are likely to be** reliable. They should give us **an approximate/the exact** amount of milk powder that will be exported from New Zealand.

8 The robustness check **shows/suggests** that the predictions **are not/may not be** entirely accurate.

9 The model is robust, **proving/suggesting** that any predictions will **probably/ definitely** be reliable.

10 The value of the residual is **about/exactly** the actual value minus the model value.

11 Forecasts beyond two cycles from the final piece of data **are less likely to be/will not be** reliable.

ISBN: 9780170472975

Pick the errors

The following statements have errors or significant omissions. Identify these.

1 **a** The average seasonal effect for the second quarter is 144 010 tonnes of apples.

b The average seasonal effect for the fourth quarter is –84 477 tonnes of apples below the trend.

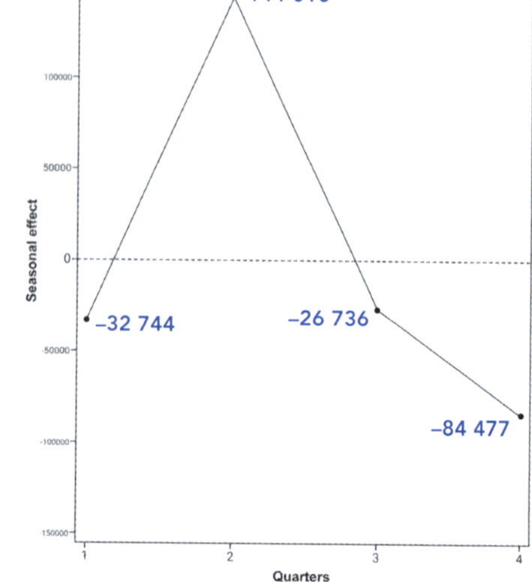

2 The predicted number of deaths in New Zealand during the first quarter of 2023 is 8297.9.

3 The last predicted value doesn't fall within the confidence intervals, so this model is not robust and the forecast cannot be relied upon.

4 This shows that the further we predict into the future, the wider the confidence interval becomes. This means the predictions become less reliable.

5 We can be 95% confident that the number of meningococcal cases in New Zealand in January of 2021 will be between –10 and 9.

Time	Min	Prediction	Max
2021M01	–10.813	–0.80634	9.2531
2021M02	–18.174	–3.3207	9.4054
2021M03	–16.58	0.82405	17.042
2021M04	–22.498	–1.8461	17.438

6 There is an average decrease in the monthly amount of sugar and sugar confectionery imported into New Zealand of 2562.5 per year.

7 There is an overall increase in the trend for the number of deaths in New Zealand from 7620 at the start of 2014 to 8970 in late 2021.

ISBN: 9780170472975

Putting it all together

The following are the **requirements** for a basic report. These have been numbered in the report below.

1. Research your context
2. Select a suitable variable that is informed by contextual knowledge
3. State the purpose of your investigation and who would find it useful
4. Describe and quantify the trend
5. Describe and quantify the seasonality
6. Make a forecast in context
7. Communicate findings in a conclusion

Improving your report

A Looking at the data more closely and researching your findings

B Forecast reliability

C Comparing variables

D Developing understanding of Holt-Winters model

E Looking into another model (multiplicative)

F Splitting the data into phases

ISBN: 9780170472975

Time series data for Campylobacter cases in New Zealand between 2016 and 2021

I am going to investigate the incidence of Campylobacter infections in the New Zealand population. The data comes from http://www.nzpho.org.nz/NotifiableDisease.aspx. The variable is the number of cases of Campylobacter per month.

I am going to investigate this because Campylobacter is a major cause of gastro-intestinal upsets (food poisoning). 'Campylobacteriosis is the most frequently notified disease in New Zealand.' (https://www.health.govt.nz/our-work/diseases-and-conditions/communicable-disease-control-manual/campylobacteriosis)

'Campylobacter is a bacterium transmitted mainly by eating contaminated food or having contact with farm animals, including dogs and cats. Infection rates are strongly linked to temperature and tend to peak in summer.' (http://www.stats. govt.nz/browse_for_stats/environment/environmental-reporting-series/environmentalindicators/Home/Atmosphere-and-climate/food-water-borne-diseases.aspx)

1 Context researched.

The history of Campylobacter incidence in New Zealand is significant: it 'started rising in New Zealand in the mid-1980s and peaked in 2006 with 15,873 notified cases.' This gave New Zealand 'the highest rate reported internationally for this disease at 384 cases per 100,000 population.' (http://www.otago.ac.nz/news/news/otago018240.html)

2 Select suitabl variable.

I would like to find out how the incidence of Campylobacter cases changed since 2016, and what the incidence likely to be in 2022. My research suggests that it is important for medical authorities to know the numbers of cases that are likely to occur, so they can be sure that they do not revert to the pre-2008 numbers. Also, by monitoring numbers, they can identify outbreaks and find the causes.

3 Purpose.

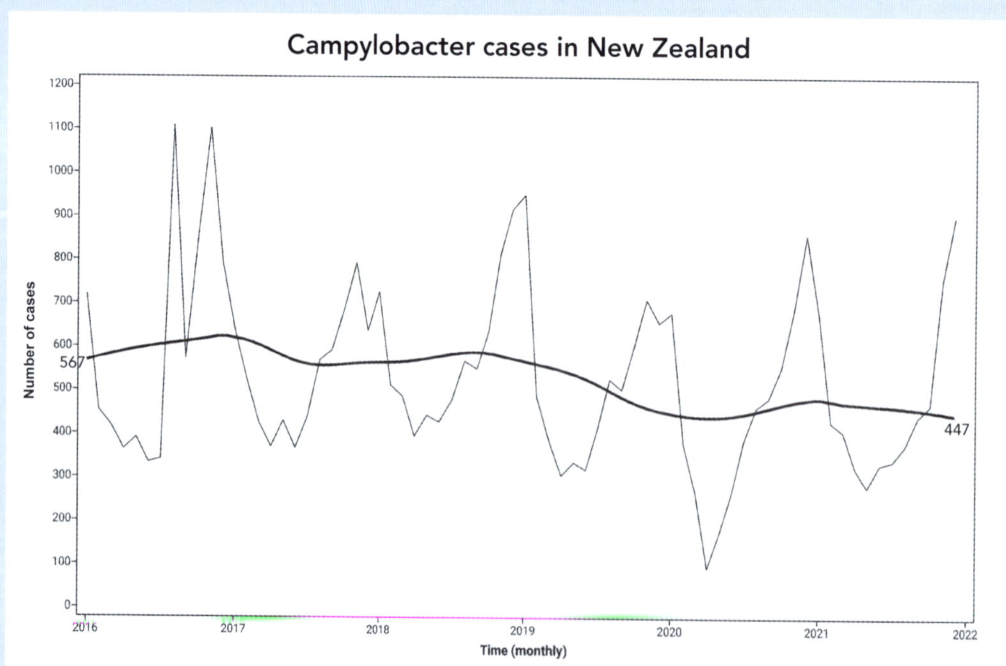

Overall, the trend for the number of Campylobacter cases has decreased from 567 cases per month at the start of 2016, to 447 cases per month at the end of 2021.

4 Trend described and quantified.

 ISBN: 9780170472975

The number of case numbers has steadily decreased over the six years and was continuing to slowly decrease in 2021.

The average decrease in the number of Campylobacter cases in New Zealand is 20 per year. This represents a reduction of approximately 3% per year. This is probably the result of an action plan which was put into place by MPI in 2007.

A Looking at the data more closely.

https://www.mpi.govt.nz/science/food-safety-and-suitability-research/campylobacter-risk-management/#:~:text=We're%20aiming%20to%20reduce,Action%20Plan%20for%20 2020%2D2021

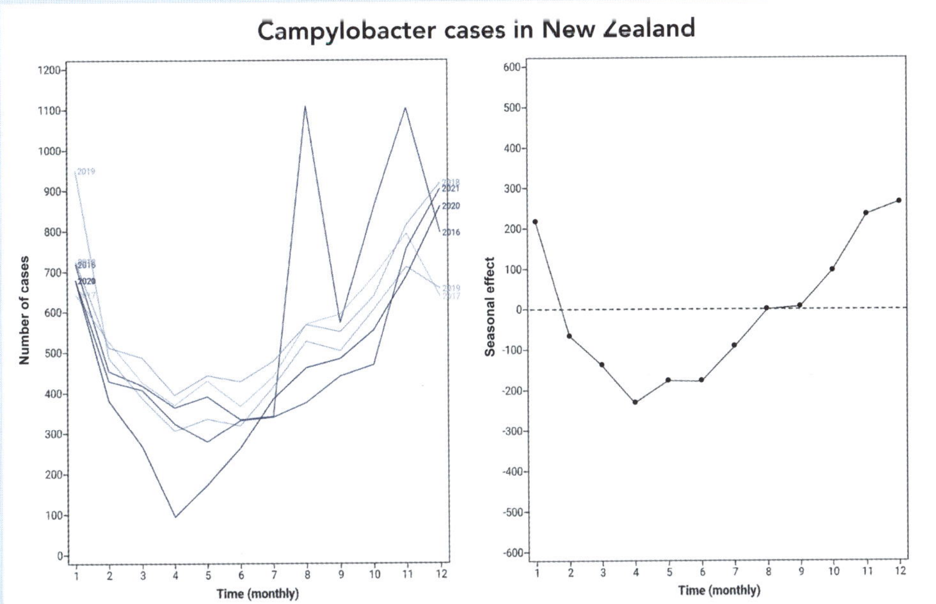

The seasonal pattern is reasonably consistent apart from late 2016 and April 2020. The number of campylobacteriosis cases peaks in December with around 264 cases above the average. The number drops until April when it is at its lowest, at around 230 cases below the average. Apart from a small decrease in June, it rises steadily throughout the rest of the year until December.

5 Seasonality quantified and discussed in context.

The high levels of Campylobacter at the start and end of the year are not surprising, as it is often caught from contaminated food, and as quoted earlier, 'Infection rates are strongly linked to temperature and tend to peak in summer'. The other reason may be that many people go on holiday in January, and that often involves camping without adequate refrigeration for food.

In August 2016, there is a clear spike in the data. This can be explained by contaminated water in Havelock North. (https://www.nzherald.co.nz/nz/havelock-north-the-new-zealand-town-where-residents-fear-the-water/XTP2GTPSVUJA4D5A7ETVLSMAFQ/)

A Findings researched.

Cases in April 2020 were at an all-time low and numbers over the following few months remained lower than usual. This was probably due to the Covid lockdown and subsequent limitations on operations of restaurants. (https://www.mpi.govt.nz/dmsdocument/47986-Annual-report-concerning-Foodborne-Diseases-in-New-Zealand-2020-Report)

Forecasts

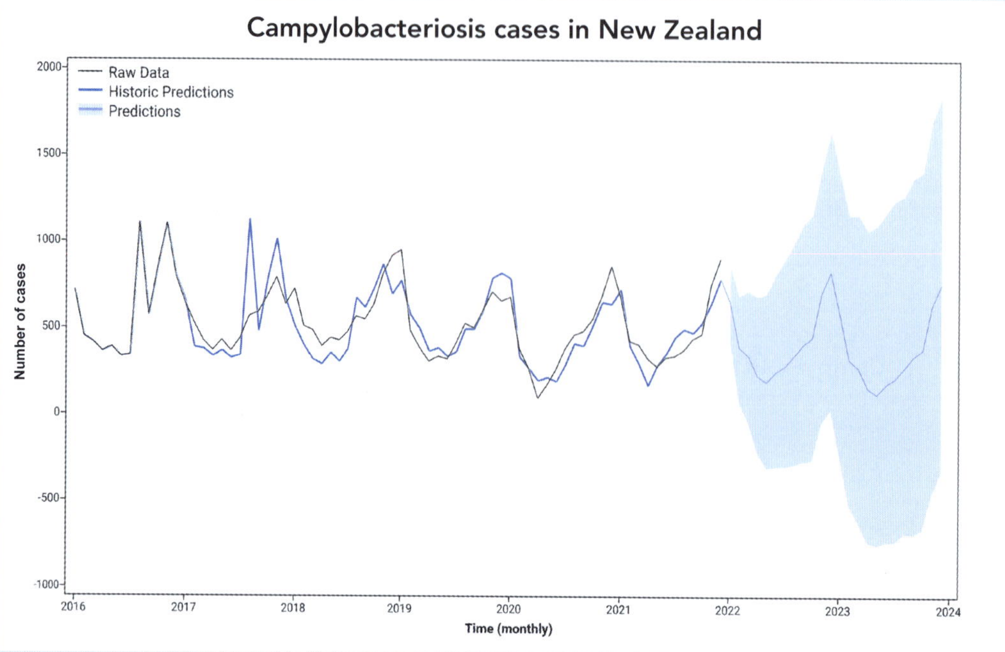

Time	Min	Prediction	Max
2022M01	428.75	651.41	860.68
2022M02	64.964	389.91	691.2
2022M03	–63.623	340.25	749.19
2022M04	–270.21	223.55	652.76
2022M05	–362.37	187.68	656.06
2022M06	–3.16.1	245.1	781.32
2022M07	–351.89	278.96	870.97
2022M08	–315.35	339.13	974.95
2022M09	–274.5	405.75	1061.6
2022M10	–273.01	447.8	1168.6
2022M11	–45.605	703.18	1457.6
2021M12	82.793	826.3	1593.1
2023M01	–197.59	571.2	1372.2
2023M02	–479.87	319.7	1107.4
2023M03	–559.38	270.04	1095.5
2023M04	–705.97	153.34	1036.8
2023M05	–753.95	117.47	1003.7
2023M06	–729.63	174.89	1110.2
2023M07	–68047	208.75	1157.7
2023M08	–635.96	268.91	1252.4
2023M09	–567.35	335.54	1346.4
2023M10	–541.11	377.59	1350.0
2023M11	–336.47	632.97	1687
2023M12	–239.13	756.09	1765.8

The forecast is for the number of Campylobacter cases during January 2022 to be around 651. We can be 95% confident that the actual number of cases in January 2022 will be between 429 and 861.

6 Forecast in context.

Although the confidence intervals become larger later in 2022 and in 2023, we can still be 95% confident that forecasts will lie between them. Some of the minimum values are negative because the confidence intervals become large relative to the predicted number of cases.

D Holt-Winters understandin

Where the minimum values are negative, the lower limit of the confidence interval is considered to be 0.

 ISBN: 9780170472975

Robustness check

Time	Min	Prediction	Max
2021M01	458.7	685.49	916312
2021M02	50.656	372.99	696.06
2021M03	–118.93	261.32	659.28
2021M04	–313.73	107.76	561
2021M05	–290.02	190.19	399.29
2021M06	–256.02	266.34	839.76
2021M07	–218.93	374.22	990.97
2021M08	–181.79	447.68	1094.2
2021M09	–201.19	455.76	1147.9
2021M10	–179.34	521.93	1232
2021M11	–93.112	648.05	1415.4
2021M12	–33.221	775.82	1584.6

Time	Campylobacteriosis	
2021M01	680	✓
2021M02	429	✓
2021M03	407	✓
2021M04	324	✓
2021M05	279	✓
2021M06	332	✓
2021M07	340	✓
2021M08	376	✓
2021M09	441	✓
2021M10	469	✓
2021M11	756	✓
2021M12	903	✓

All twelve values lie within the confidence intervals. This, along with the consistent seasonal pattern and the reasonably steady trend, suggests that we can be fairly confident in the forecasts.

B Forecast reliability.

Comparison

This graph shows the number of cases of both Campylobacter and Salmonella in New Zealand.

C Comparing with another variable.

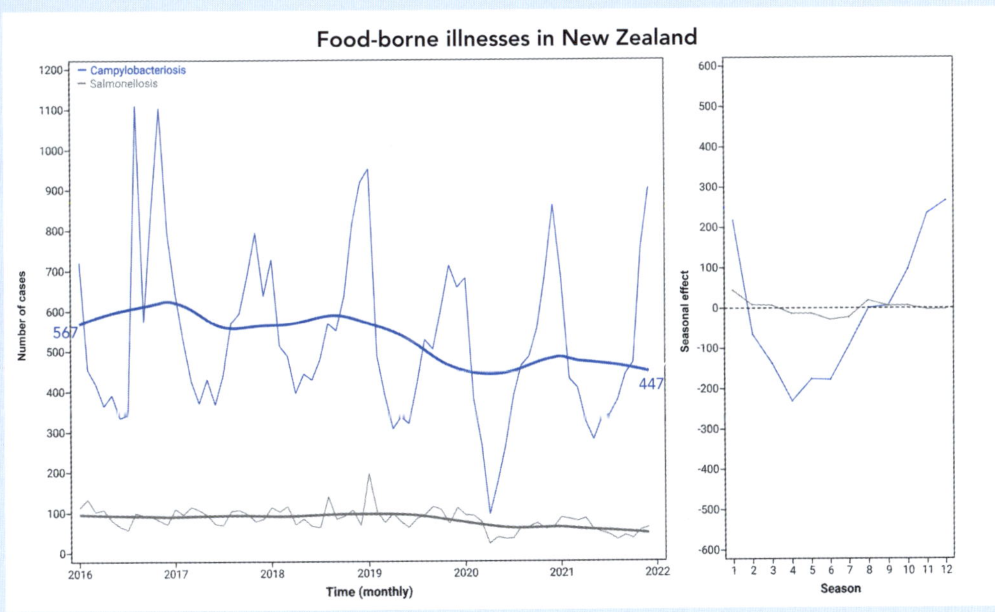

The trends for both illnesses show a similar pattern, in that they have both gradually decreased between 2016 and 2022. There are far more cases of Campylobacter than Salmonella in New Zealand, and its incidence is more influenced by the seasons.

ISBN: 9780170472975

Conclusion

The number of cases of Campylobacter in New Zealand has generally decreased from 2016 until 2021. While Food Safe New Zealand has a goal to reduce the amount of Campylobacter by 20% by 2025, our forecasts suggest that it is unlikely to hit this target.

Camplyobacter infections are more common in summer when the temperatures are higher, and less common during the cooler months.

The forecast made for 2022 should be reliable and would be useful for health authorities for monitoring levels of infection so they can adjust their goal or re-evaluate any measures they have in place.

This study was restricted to New Zealand data. It would be interesting to compare this with data from other countries, and to see what interventions have been successful in reducing the cases of Campylobacter.

7 Conclusion.

ISBN: 9780170472975

Practice tasks

Practice task one

Find the seven major mistakes or omissions from this report. Identify them and write a corrected version of each.

I will investigate how many ice creams were sold in Springview Dairy over the past three years. This will allow the owner to know how much profit they are going to make in the future. The owner would be interested to see the findings of this report. February has been labelled 'ice cream month'. (https://www.fmcgbusiness.co.nz/its-nz-ice-cream-month/)

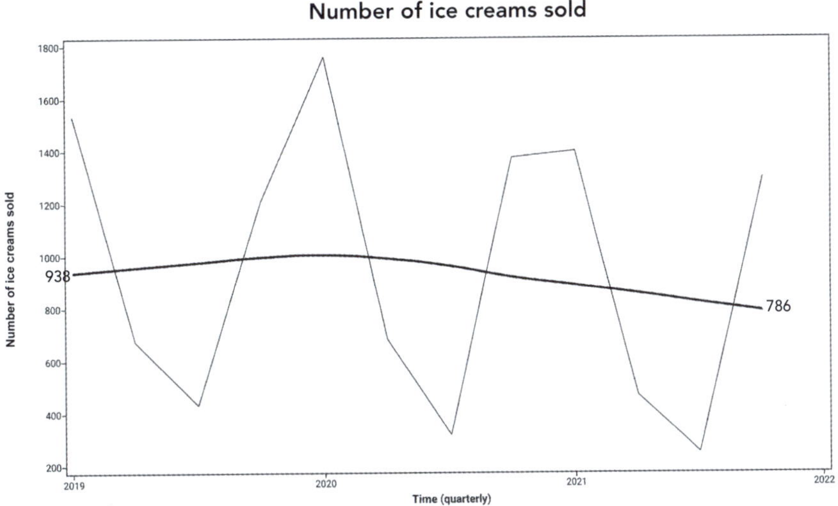

The trend shows a seasonal pattern in which more ice creams are sold in summer and fewer in winter. There has been an overall increase in the trend of ice cream sales from 938 per month at the start of 2019 to 786 per quarter towards the end of 2021. The number of ice creams sold increased slightly during 2019, but has decreased over the last two years.

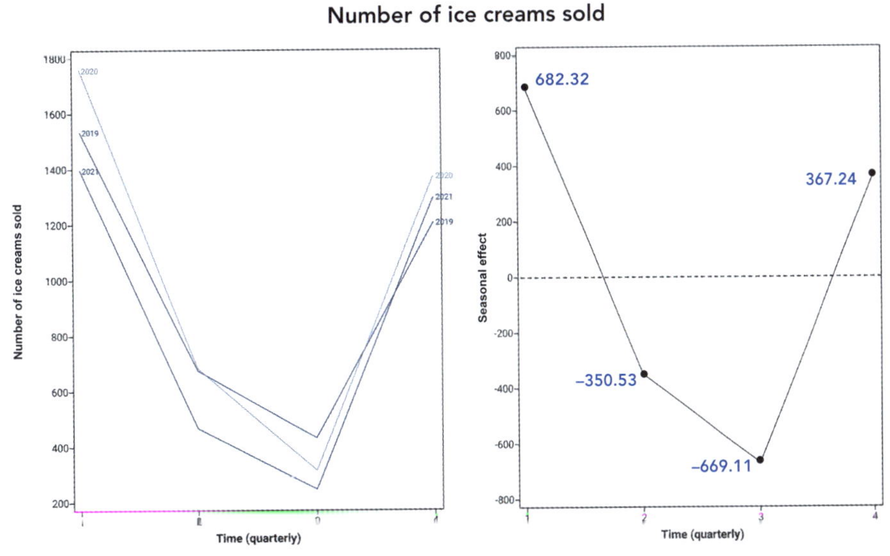

We can see the seasonal pattern is the same each year. The first quarter of ice cream sales is the highest and the third quarter is lowest with about –669 below average. This means more ice creams are sold in spring and summer.

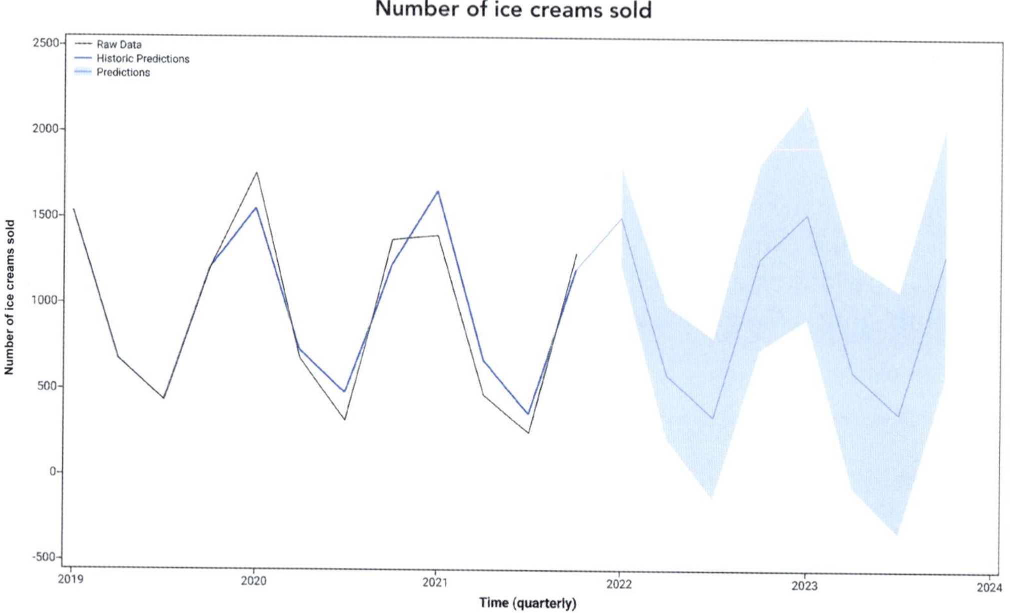

The number of ice creams sold at Springview Dairy in the first quarter of 2022 is predicted to be approximately 1240.

Time	Min	Prediction	Max
2022Q1	1239.7	1511.5	1767.1
2022Q2	193.27	592.85	966.83
2022Q3	–138.98	345.8	793.01
2022Q4	711.51	1269.6	1792.4
2023Q1	869.6	1532.3	2150.2
2023Q2	–106.04	613.7	1303.9
2023Q3	–383.48	366.65	1074.3
2023Q4	469.09	1290.4	2044.3

In conclusion, Springview Dairy should buy more ice creams in Quarter 4 and Quarter 1. It looks as though ice cream sales will continue to decrease slightly, although this might change if we have some really hot weather.

ISBN: 9780170472975

Practice task two

Introduction

This activity requires you to investigate how much is spent on groceries per quarter in New Zealand, including making a forecast, and to write a report on your findings.

Your overall grade will be determined by how well you carry out your investigation and how well you apply the statistical enquiry cycle.

Task

You have been given graphs for the total amounts spent on groceries per quarter in New Zealand, in millions of dollars.

The data is listed on page 94 and an electronic version of this data can be found at https://cengage.co.nz/product/isbn/9780170389402.

Use the statistical enquiry cycle to carry out a statistical investigation to determine patterns in grocery spending. Write a report describing the investigation.

1 Familiarise yourself with the data set provided. This will include doing research to help you understand the variable and to develop a purpose for the investigation.
2 Identify features in the data and relate these to the context.
3 Find appropriate model(s).
4 Use model(s) to make forecast(s).
5 Write a conclusion. Support your conclusion by referring to your analysis and/or features of the visual display(s). Include a reflection on your process, which could consider other relevant variables, an evaluation of the adequacy of the model(s), consideration of the validity of your forecast(s), or a deeper understanding of the model(s).

In writing your report, link your discussion to the context and support the statements you make by referring to statistical evidence.

ISBN: 9780170472975

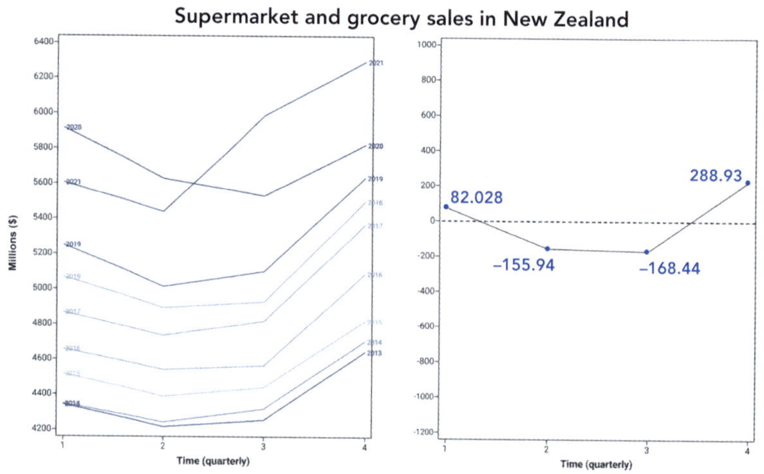

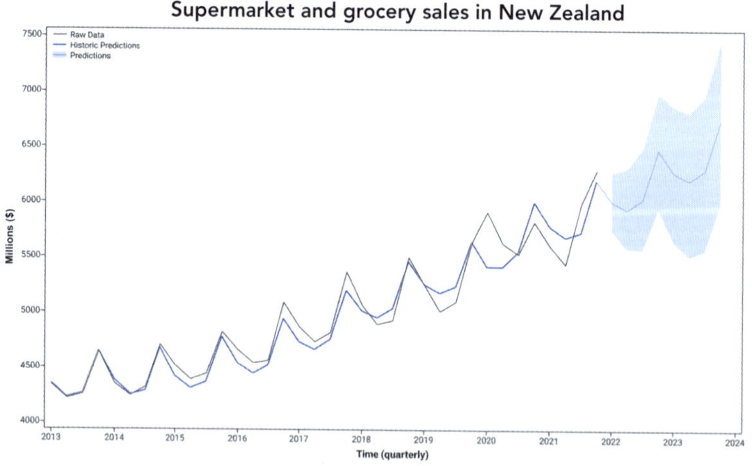

Time	Min	Prediction	Max
2022Q1	5754.1	6010.2	6271.8
2022Q2	5538.9	5939.5	6311.2
2022Q3	5541	6034.6	6457.1
2022Q4	5915.8	6480.2	6986
2023Q1	5658.5	6274.8	6885.5
2023Q2	5542.9	6204.1	6869.6
2023Q3	5585.4	6299.2	6970.2
2023Q4	5979.9	6744.8	7465

ISBN: 9780170472975

Research and variable

Purpose

Trend

ISBN: 9780170472975

Seasonality

Forecast

Conclusion

 ISBN: 9780170472975

Practice task three

Introduction

This activity requires you to investigate the availability of alcohol in New Zealand. The variables are beer, spirits and wine. The values are in millions of litres.

Task

You have been given graphs for the quarterly amount of alcohol available for consumption in New Zealand from 2012 until 2021.

The data is listed on page 94 and an electronic version of this data can be found at https://cengage.co.nz/product/isbn/9780170389402.

Use the statistical enquiry cycle to carry out a statistical investigation to determine patterns in alcohol consumption. Write a report describing the investigation.

1. Familiarise yourself with the data set provided. This will include doing research to help you understand the variables and to develop a purpose for the investigation.
2. Select at least one of the variables to investigate.
3. Identify features in the data and relate these to the context.
4. Find appropriate model(s).
5. Use model(s) to make forecast(s).
6. Write a conclusion. Support your conclusion by referring to your analysis and/or features of the visual display(s). Include a reflection on your process, which could consider other relevant variables, an evaluation of the adequacy of the model(s), consideration of the validity of your forecast(s), or a deeper understanding of the model(s).

In writing your report, link your discussion to the context and support the statements you make by referring to statistical evidence.

Beer

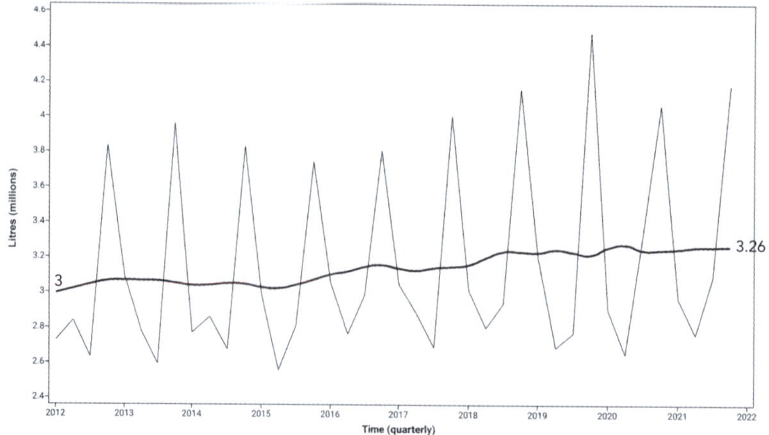

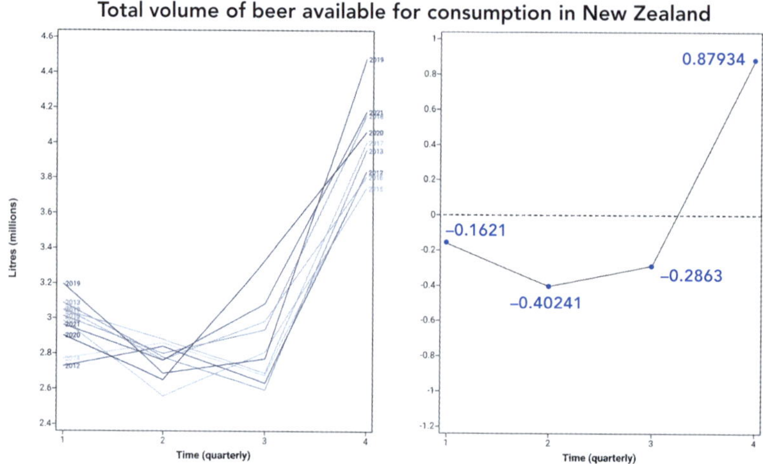

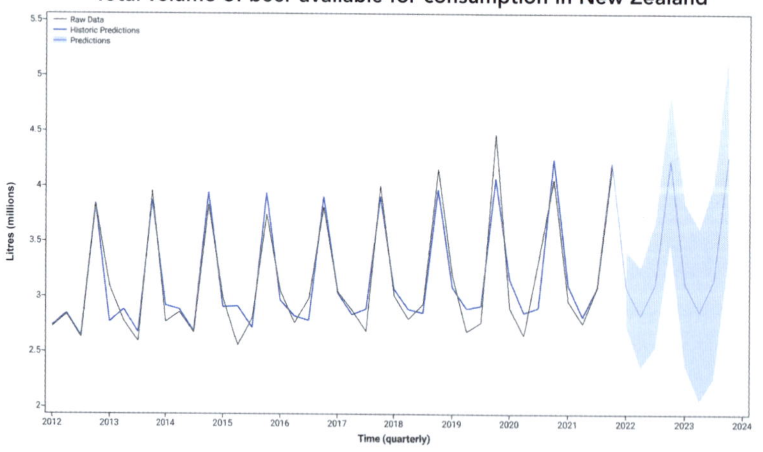

Time	Min	Prediction	Max
2022Q1	2.7795	3.0923	3.4139
2022Q2	2.3442	2.8348	3.2876
2022Q3	2.5728	3.1219	3.7173
2022Q4	3.6118	4.2406	4.9188
2023Q1	2.3923	3.1268	3.8575
2023Q2	2.0824	2.8694	3.657
2023Q3	2.2767	3.1565	4.0409
2023Q4	3.3669	4.2751	5.1491

ISBN: 9780170472975

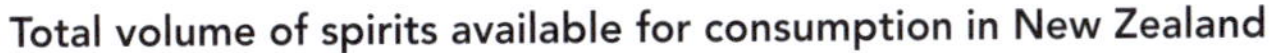

Spirits

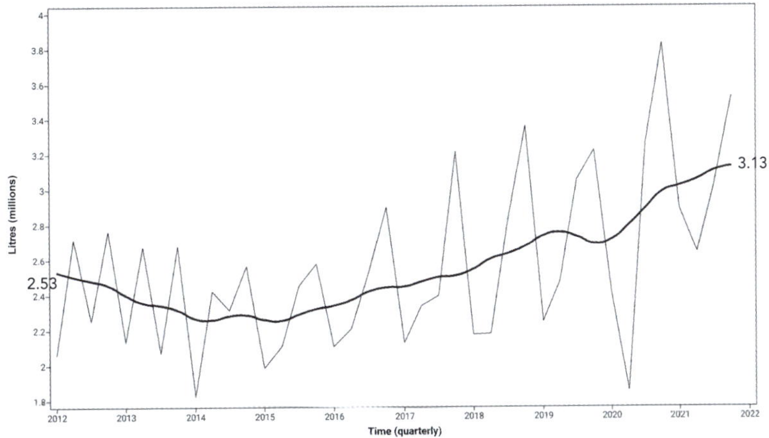

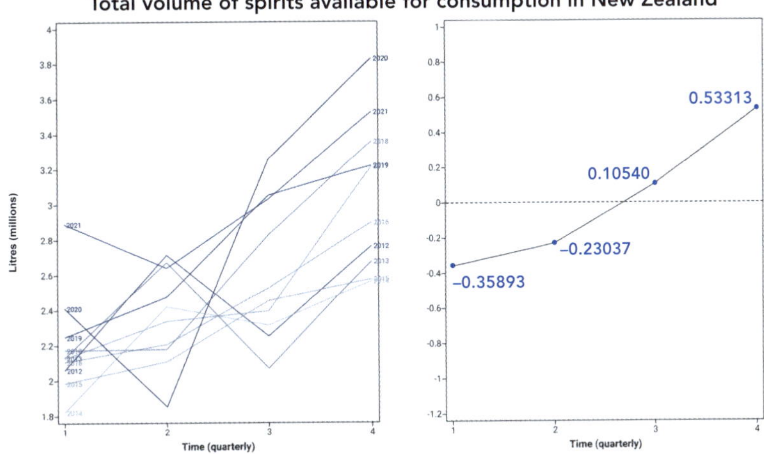

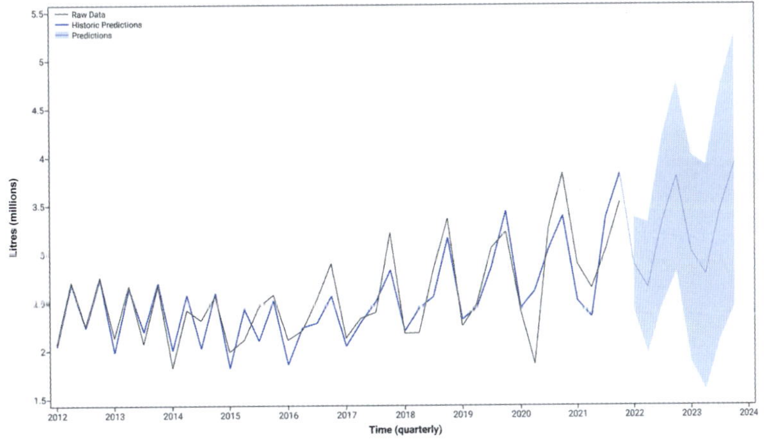

Time	Min	Prediction	Max
2022Q1	2.3915	2.885	3.3613
2022Q2	1.9543	2.6459	3.3586
2022Q3	2.5145	3.3112	4.1827
2022Q4	2.7458	3.7943	4.7829
2023Q1	1.9147	3.0192	4.1085
2023Q2	1.5826	2.7801	3.9536
2023Q3	2.1485	3.4454	4.7158
2023Q4	2.5189	3.9285	5.3069

ISBN: 9780170472975

Wine

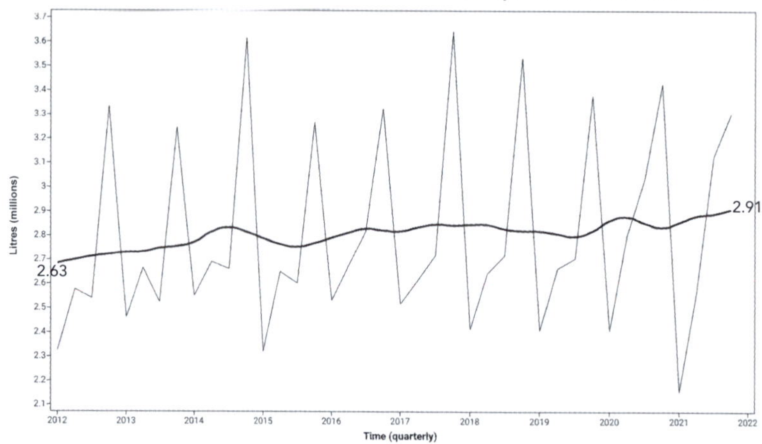

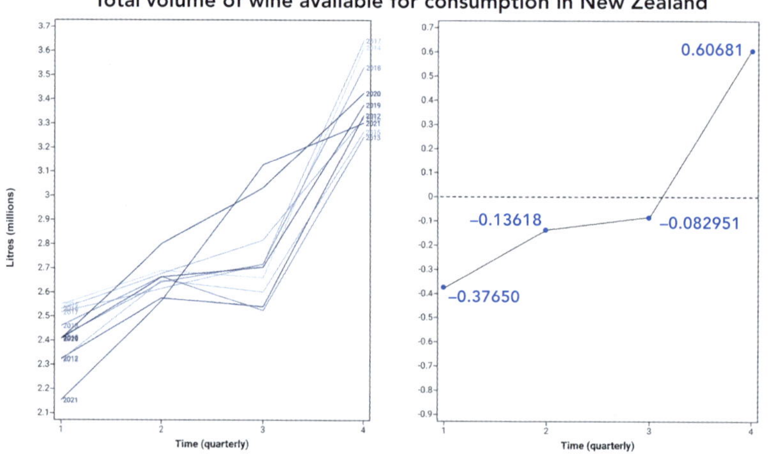

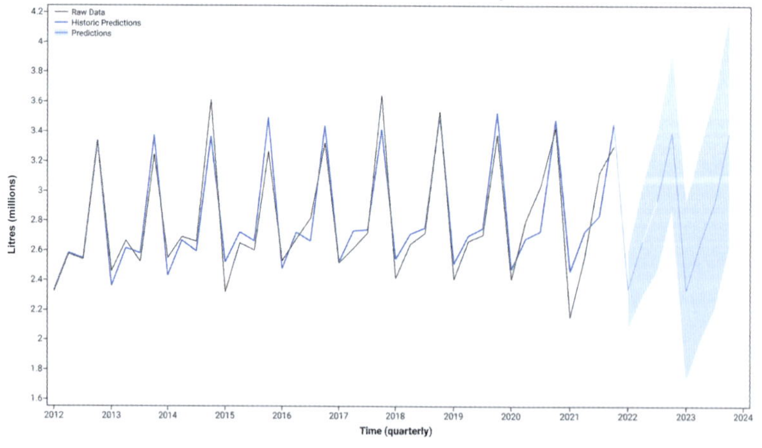

Time	Min	Prediction	Max
2022Q1	2.0723	2.3428	2.6004
2022Q2	2.2871	2.6657	3.0287
2022Q3	2.5	2.9346	3.4533
2022Q4	2.8555	3.3949	3.9494
2023Q1	1.7309	2.3363	2.9357
2023Q2	2.0055	2.6592	3.2777
2023Q3	2.1952	2.928	3.6109
2023Q4	2.5992	3.3883	4.0934

ISBN: 9780170472975

Research and choice of variable

Purpose

Trend

Seasonality

Forecast

Conclusion

ISBN: 9780170472975

Data sources

Deaths and births: **http://infoshare.stats.govt.nz/**

ESR notifiable diseases: **https://www.esr.cri.nz/our-services/consultancy/public-health/notifiable-diseases-intelligence-dashboard/**

Crimes and offences: **https://www.police.govt.nz**

The total number of nights per quarter spent by domestic (New Zealand) guests in hotels and motels in Canterbury: **http://www.stats.govt.nz/infoshare/**

The total number of nights per quarter spent by international guests in hotels and motels in Canterbury: **http://www.stats.govt.nz/infoshare/**

Divorces in New Zealand: **http://infoshare.stats.govt.nz/**

Cattle, pig and sheep slaughtered in New Zealand: **http://infoshare.stats.govt.nz/**

Exports of kiwifruit, apples and milk powder: **http://infoshare.stats.govt.nz/**

The total number of guest nights available per year in hotels and motels in Canterbury: **http://www.stats.govt.nz/infoshare/**

Imports of sugar and sugar confectionery: **http://infoshare.stats.govt.nz/**

Births in New Zealand: **http://infoshare.stats.govt.nz/**

Number of court proceedings in New Zealand: **https://www.police.govt.nz**

The total number of passenger movements in and out of New Zealand each quarter: **http://www.stats.govt.nz/infoshare/**

Supermarket and grocery sales in New Zealand: **http://infoshare.stats.govt.nz/**

Volume of alcohol avaliable for consumption in New Zealand: **http://infoshare.stats.govt.nz/**

Graphs

Graphs have been modified from NZGrapher (**https://www.jake4maths.com/grapher/**)

ISBN: 9780170472975

Practice task two data

(page 84)

Total amounts spent on groceries per quarter in New Zealand, in millions of dollars.

Time	Grocery sales
2013Q1	4342.70
2013Q2	4216.20
2013Q3	4255.50
2013Q4	4645.30
2014Q1	4348.10
2014Q2	4242.50
2014Q3	4319.00
2014Q4	4706.10
2015Q1	4516.00
2015Q2	4388.70
2015Q3	4441.10
2015Q4	4820.60
2016Q1	4657.50
2016Q2	4540.20
2016Q3	4564.00
2016Q4	5090.90
2017Q1	4867.90
2017Q2	4734.40
2017Q3	4818.60
2017Q4	5368.40
2018Q1	5067.80
2018Q2	4892.90
2018Q3	4927.60
2018Q4	5499.70
2019Q1	5250.00
2019Q2	5013.20
2019Q3	5100.80
2019Q4	5636.90
2020Q1	5915.40
2020Q2	5627.90
2020Q3	5529.40
2020Q4	5823.50
2021Q1	5605.90
2021Q2	5438.00
2021Q3	5986.50
2021Q4	6294.60

Practice task three data

(pages 88–90)

The quarterly amount of alcohol available for consumption in New Zealand, in millions of litres.

Year	Beer	Spirits	Wine
2012Q1	2.728	2.061	2.325
2012Q2	2.84	2.715	2.577
2012Q3	2.633	2.252	2.54
2012Q4	3.837	2.764	3.335
2013Q1	3.09	2.132	2.461
2013Q2	2.779	2.673	2.666
2013Q3	2.594	2.07	2.524
2013Q4	3.96	2.677	3.246
2014Q1	2.771	1.823	2.55
2014Q2	2.86	2.421	2.691
2014Q3	2.676	2.314	2.661
2014Q4	3.831	2.564	3.616
2015Q1	2.986	1.986	2.32
2015Q2	2.558	2.109	2.65
2015Q3	2.81	2.453	2.602
2015Q4	3.743	2.576	3.268
2016Q1	3.054	2.107	2.531
2016Q2	2.764	2.207	2.678
2016Q3	2.985	2.526	2.817
2016Q4	3.807	2.898	3.324
2017Q1	3.046	2.127	2.517
2017Q2	2.88	2.338	2.616
2017Q3	2.689	2.395	2.718
2017Q4	4.005	3.215	3.644
2018Q1	3.013	2.174	2.413
2018Q2	2.8	2.179	2.643
2018Q3	2.937	2.828	2.717
2018Q4	4.158	3.358	3.534
2019Q1	3.197	2.248	2.408
2019Q2	2.687	2.476	2.664
2019Q3	2.771	3.053	2.705
2019Q4	4.478	3.221	3.379
2020Q1	2.903	2.412	2.407
2020Q2	2.65	1.853	2.801
2020Q3	3.332	3.258	3.033
2020Q4	4.064	3.829	3.427
2021Q1	2.964	2.891	2.154
2021Q2	2.761	2.641	2.564
2021Q3	3.087	3.031	3.128
2021Q4	4.178	3.526	3.304

ISBN: 9780170472975

Answers

The mathematics behind time series (pp. 8–20)

The trend (pp. 9–13)

Year	Number of pies sold
2013	2690
2014	3094
2015	3751
2016	3631
2017	3612
2018	3871
2019	3545
2020	4125
2021	4607

Working and moving mean	Trend (year, moving mean)
= 3178	(2014, 3178)
= 3492	(2015, 3492)
$\frac{3751 + 3631 + 3612}{3} = 3665$	(2016, 3665)
$\frac{3631 + 3612 + 3871}{3} = 3705$	(2017, 3705)
$\frac{3612 + 3871 + 3545}{3} = 3676$	(2018, 3676)
$\frac{3871 + 3545 + 4125}{3} = 3847$	(2019, 3847)
$\frac{3545 + 4125 + 4607}{3} = 4092$	(2020, 4092)

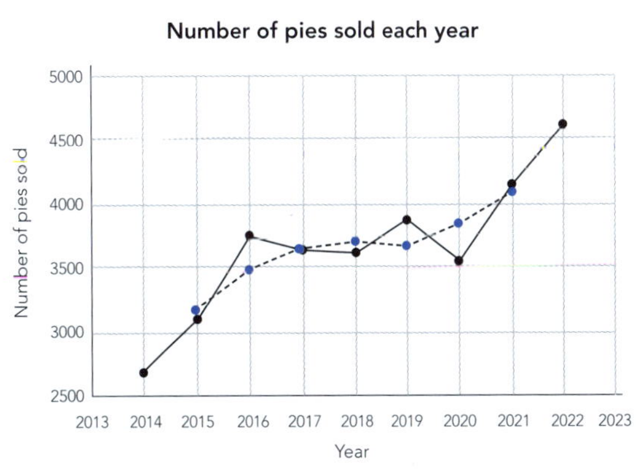

Year	Quarter	Number of pies sold	Working	Moving mean (4)	Working	Centred moving mean (CMM)	Trend (year, CMM)
2019	Q1	528					
	Q2	1192					
			$= \frac{528 + 1192 + 1360 + 465}{4}$	886.25			
	Q3	1360			$\frac{886.25 + 888.5}{2}$	887	(2019 Q3, 887)
			$= \frac{1192 + 1360 + 465 + 537}{4}$	888.5			
	Q4	465			$\frac{888.5 + 935.25}{2}$	912	(2019 Q4, 912)
			$= \frac{1360 + 465 + 537 + 1379}{4}$	935.25			
2020	Q1	537			$\frac{935.25 + 999.5}{2}$	967	(2020 Q1, 967)
			$= \frac{465 + 537 + 1379 + 1617}{4}$	999.5			
	Q2	1379			$\frac{999.5 + 1031.25}{2}$	1015	(2020 Q2, 1015)
			$= \frac{537 + 1379 + 1617 + 592}{4}$	1031.25			
	Q3	1617			$\frac{1031.25 + 1053.25}{2}$	1042	(2020 Q3, 1042)
			$= \frac{1379 + 1617 + 592 + 625}{4}$	1053.25			
	Q4	592			$\frac{1053.25 + 1121.25}{2}$	1087	(2020 Q4, 1087)
			$= \frac{1617 + 592 + 625 + 1651}{4}$	1121.25			
2021	Q1	625			$\frac{1121.25 + 1144.25}{2}$	1133	(2021 Q1, 1132)
			$= \frac{592 + 625 + 1651 + 1709}{4}$	1144.25			
	Q2	1651			$\frac{1144.25 + 1151.75}{2}$	1148	(2021 Q2, 1148)
			$= \frac{625 + 1651 + 1709 + 622}{4}$	1151.75			
	Q3	1709					
	Q4	622					

ISBN: 9780170472975

Number of pies sold per quarter

1800
1600
1400
1200
1000
800
600
400

Number of pies sold

Q1 Q2 Q3 Q4 Q1 Q2 Q3 Q4 Q1 Q2 Q3 Q4
2019 2020 2021

Years and quarters

The seasonal pattern (pp. 14–15)

Year	Quarter	Number of pies sold	CMM	Working	Individual seasonal effect
2019	Q1	528			
	Q2	1192			
	Q3	1360	887	1360 – 887	473
	Q4	465	912	465 – 912	–447
2020	Q1	537	967	**537 – 967**	–430
	Q2	1379	1015	**1379 – 1015**	**364**
	Q3	1617	1042	**1617 – 1042**	**575**
	Q4	592	1087	**592 – 1087**	**–495**
2021	Q1	625	1133	**625 – 1133**	**–508**
	Q2	1651	1148	**1651 – 1148**	**503**
	Q3	1709			
	Q4	622			

Season	Working	Average seasonal effect
Q1	$\frac{(-460) + (-508)}{2}$	–469
Q2	$\frac{364 + 503}{2}$	434
Q3	$\frac{473 + 575}{2}$	**524**
Q4	$\frac{(-477) + (-495)}{2}$	**–471**

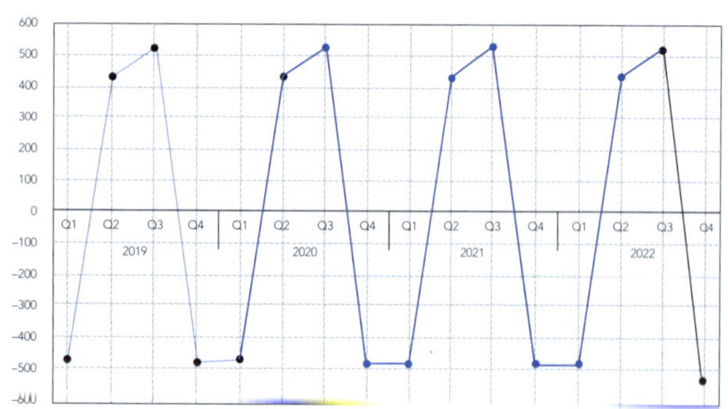

The model (pp. 16–17)

Year	Quarter	Number of pies sold	CMM	Average seasonal effect	Working	Recomposed data (the model)
2019	Q1	528				
	Q2	1192				
	Q3	1360	887	524	887 + 524	1411
	Q4	465	912	–471	912 + (–471)	441
2020	Q1	537	967	–469	**967 + (–469)**	498
	Q2	1379	1015	434	**1015 + 434**	1449
	Q3	1617	1042	524	**1042 + 524**	**1566**
	Q4	592	1087	–471	**1087 + (–471)**	**616**
2021	Q1	625	1133	–469	**1133 + (–469)**	**664**
	Q2	1651	1148	434	**1148 + 434**	**1582**
	Q3	1709				
	Q4	622				

Forecasts (p. 18)

Year	Quarter	Extended trend	Average seasonal effect	Working	Forecasts
2022	Q1	1281	–469	1281 + (–469)	812
	Q2	1320	434	**1320 + 434**	1754
	Q3	1359	524	**1359 + 524**	**1883**
	Q4	1399	–471	**1399 + (–471)**	**928**

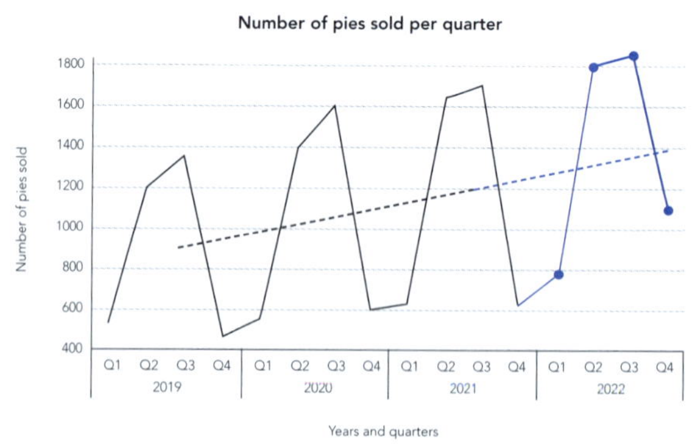

 ISBN: 9780170472975

Unusual points (pp. 19–20)

Year	Quarter	Number of pies sold	CMM	Average seasonal effect	Working	Residuals
2019	Q1	528				
	Q2	1192				
	Q3	1360	887	524	1360 – (887 + 524)	–51
	Q4	465	912	–471	465 – (912 + (–471))	24
2020	Q1	537	967	–469	**537 – (967 + (–469))**	**39**
	Q2	1379	1015	434	**1379 – (1015 + 434)**	**–70**
	Q3	1617	1042	524	**1617 – (1042 + 524)**	**51**
	Q4	592	1087	–471	**592 – (1087 + (–471))**	**–24**
2021	Q1	625	1133	–469	**625 – (1133 + (–469))**	**–39**
	Q2	1651	1148	434	**1651 – (1148 + 434)**	**69**
	Q3	1709				
	Q4	622				

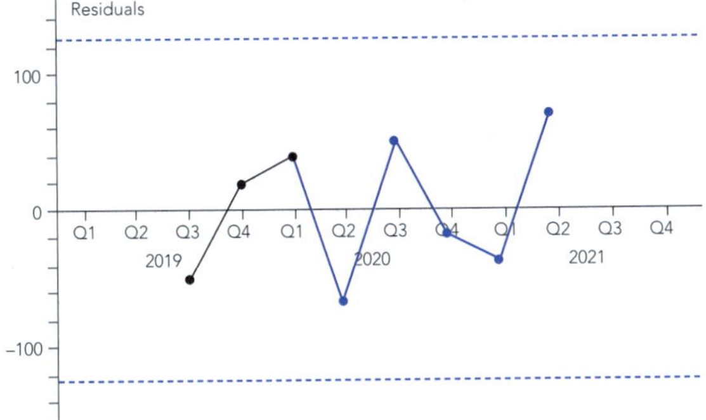

Note: The answers from here on may not be exhaustive. If your answers are different, check them with your teacher.

Requirements of a basic report (pp. 21–43)

1 Research your context (p. 21)

1 a What are salmonellosis and campylobacteriosis?
Are they an issue in New Zealand?
How are they contracted?
Who might be interested in the forecasted numbers? What use could they have?

b What are the common causes of death in New Zealand?
What age group is most common?

2 Select a suitable variable that is informed by contextual knowledge (pp. 22–23)

1 Not really enough data to be confident in conclusions.
2 No seasonality, which will limit your report.
3 Not a lot to talk about; the seasonality seems consistent and the trend isn't increasing or decreasing.

3 State the purpose of your investigation and who would find it useful (pp. 24–25)

1 Why might we investigate this?
Kiwi fruit is a major export for New Zealand, and a major economic contributor to the nation.
Who might be interested?
Kiwifruit growers, the Ministry for Primary Industries, exporters.
What might you research?
How much is the kiwifruit industry worth to New Zealand?
How much are sales to the domestic market worth compared with the worth of exports?
What time of year do we export kiwifruit?
Do any other countries grow and export kiwifruit, and at what times of the year?

2 Why might we investigate this?
To establish if there are days during the week where crimes are more likely.
Who might be interested?
Police and the community.
What might you research?
Are some crimes more likely to occur on certain days of the week?
What makes different crimes more likely?

3 Why might we investigate this?
To establish if there are times of the year when there is more supply/demand. This may lead to jobs and or expansions of business/farming sector.
Who might be interested?
Farmers, slaughterhouses, exporters, butchers.
What might you research?
What are the products from slaughtered sheep, and what happens to these products?
When is there greatest demand for these products?
What proportion of these products are exported?

4 The trend (pp. 26–32)

Describe and quantify the trend

1 a There is an overall ~~increase/~~**decrease** in the trend for the amount of sugar imported into New Zealand from **49 100** per **month** in **2014** to **28 700** per **month** in **2021**.

b From 2014 until 2019, **there is a gradual decrease followed by a gradual increase**.
During 2019, **there is a significant decrease in the amount of sugar and sugar confectionery imported into New Zealand**.
In 2020, there is a slight **increase** followed by a **decrease** during 2021.

c During 2021, the data has been **consistently decreasing**.

2 There is an overall **increase**/~~decrease~~ in the trend in births in New Zealand from **14 300** per **quarter** in **2014** to **15 500** per **quarter** in **2021**.
From 2014 until 2019, **the number of births has fluctuated**.
From 2019 until mid-2020, **the number of births decreased**.
Since mid-2020, the data has **been significantly increasing**.

ISBN: 9780170472975

3 a There is a very small increase in the number of invasive pneumococcal cases in New Zealand from 37.7 per month in 2016 to 39 per month in 2021.

b There was a very slight but steady increase in cases from the start of 2016 until a peak halfway through 2018. Since then the number of cases declined more rapidly until a low point the middle of 2021.

c Since the middle of 2021, the number of cases has been increasing.

4 There was an overall decrease in the number of court proceedings in New Zealand from 43 600 per month in mid-2014 to 26 400 court proceedings per month in 2021.
Apart from a slight peak in early 2010, there was a steady decrease from 2014 until 2020. At this point the number of court proceedings increased slightly, and then decreased at a higher rate until the end of 2021.

5 The seasonal pattern (pp. 33–37)
Describe and quantify the seasonal pattern

1 Quarter two: **There are about 144 000 tonnes of apples above average exported in quarter two.**
Quarter three: **There are almost 27 000 tonnes of apples below average exported in quarter three.**
Quarter four: **There are about 84 500 tonnes of apples below average exported in quarter four.**
Reasons: The mass of apples exported from New Zealand peaks in the second quarter as harvesting of ripe fruit occurs from February to April.

2 There is a peak of about 44 cases above/~~below~~ average in January.
From then until June, the number of salmonellosis cases reduce to about 28 below average per month in June.
From July to August, the number of cases increases steeply until there are just under 19 cases above the average per month in August.
From August onwards, the number of cases decreases to around the average.
Reasons: Salmonellosis is mainly contracted by eating contaminated food. Warmer temperatures allow the bacteria to grow faster, which explains why there is a peak in January and fewer cases in winter.

3 On Mondays and Tuesdays there are around 5000 below average number of crimes committed.
After that, the number of crimes increases until it is about 700 below the average on Thursday.
Then the number increases very steeply to about 8000 crimes above average on a Friday. It peaks on Saturday, and then very rapidly decrease to about 700 below the average on Sunday.
A higher level of crime on Fridays and Saturdays is probably attributable to the increase in alcohol consumption on these days.

4 The lowest amounts of sugar and sugar confectionery imported are during February (about 13 000 tonnes below average) and May (about 12 000 tonnes below average).
For the remaining months up until August, imports are about average. From August to October the amount of sugar and sugar confectionery imported increases to a peak in October of around 10 000 tonnes above average. In November and December the amount imported is about average.
The peak in March-April will be due to imports for Easter, and that for October are likely to be imports for the Christmas season.

6 Make a forecast in context (pp. 38–42)

1 The number of births expected in New Zealand in the first quarter of 2022 is approximately **14 653**.
We can be 95% confident that the number of births in New Zealand in Quarter 1 of 2022 will be between **13 316** and **15 996**.

2 The number of court proceedings expected in New Zealand in the first month of 2022 is approximately 27 096.
We can be 95% confident that the number of court proceedings in New Zealand in the first month of 2022 will be between 23 163 and 31 077.

3 The number of crimes expected in New Zealand on the first Monday of Week 5 is approximately 64 531.
We can be 95% confident that the number of crimes in New Zealand the first Monday of Week 5 will be between 60 529 and 68 738.

4 The number of cases of invasive pneumococcal in New Zealand in the first month of 2022 is approximately 22.
We can be 95% confident that the number of cases of invasive pneumococcal in New Zealand in Month 1 of 2022 will be between 0 and 48.

Improving your report (pp. 46–71)

A Looking at the data more closely and researching your findings (pp. 47–57)

Check answers requiring research and reasons with your teacher.

Trend

1 Calculation $= \frac{28\,700 - 49\,100}{8} = -2550$

There is an **average** ~~increase~~/**decrease** in the **monthly** amount of sugar and sugar confectionery imported into New Zealand of **2550** tonnes per **year**.
We have been unable to find reasons for this.
There is a significant decrease in 2019 and again in 2021.
There aren't any clear reasons for these decreases.

 ISBN: 9780170472975

2 Calculation = $\frac{509\,000 - 422\,000}{9}$ = **9666.67 (2 dp)**

There is an **average** increase/~~decrease~~ in **the quarterly amount of milk powder exported from New Zealand of 9666 tonnes per year**.
New Zealand's dairy production has increased during this period partly due to increased global demand. https://www.dcanz.com/about-the-nz-dairy-industry/
There are no significant increases or decreases in this data set.

3 Calculation = $\frac{26\,400 - 43\,600}{7.5}$ = –2293.33 (2 dp)

There is an average decrease in the monthly number of court proceedings in New Zealand of 2293 per year.
There is a particularly steep drop during 2020 and 2021.
This is due to the Covid pandemic because courts were unable to operate for most cases.
https://www.courtsofnz.govt.nz/the-courts/high-court/annual-statistics/annual-statistics-for-the-high-court/#:~:text=There%20were%201%2C113%20general%20proceedings,1%2C130%20cases%20filed%20last%20year.

4 Calculation = $\frac{47.6 - 95.6}{6}$ = –8

There is an average decrease in the monthly number of salmonellosis cases in New Zealand of about 8 per year.
There is a significant decrease during 2020 and 2021. This was probably due to the Covid pandemic as food businesses were shut during lockdowns, and once the lockdowns were lifted there were limitations on how food outlets could operate. In addition, many people were reluctant to eat out, particularly in enclosed spaces.

Seasonal pattern and identifying unusual seasonal values

1 Seasonal pattern: There is no clear seasonal pattern, but cases do appear to be more prevalent during the warmer months of the year.
Unusual points and explanations: There is a spike in cases in January 2019. This is confirmed by Food Safety News who report an outbreak due to chickens with Salmonella from one poultry farm.

2 Seasonal pattern: There is no clear seasonal pattern.
Unusual points and explanations: There is a spike in June 2016. No reason has been found for this.
There is a spike in March of 2020 where there were a large number of proceedings. This was probably because larger numbers than usual were pushed through the courts in anticipation of the lockdown.
After the March peak until the end of 2021, the numbers of court proceedings is much lower than normal due to Covid restrictions.
There was a peak in the number of court proceedings in June 2016. No reason has been found for this.

3 Seasonal pattern: There is a strong seasonal pattern in the number of sheep slaughtered each month. The numbers peak in January and then drop steeply until July and August when they at their lowest point. Lambs are born in the spring when there is plenty of feed, and by January, most are large enough to be killed for meat. Farmers progressively send lambs to the works during late summer in order to have low stock numbers in winter when there is limited feed. https://teara.govt.nz/en/sheep-farming/page-10
Unusual points and explanations: In April 2020, the number of sheep slaughtered was unusually low. This is because the freezing works were unable to operate during the Covid lockdown, but in the following month there were larger numbers slaughtered due to the backlog from April.
In 2021, there were fewer sheep slaughtered than usual in January and February, but these low numbers were compensated for by higher numbers in March. No particular reason was found for this.

4 Seasonal pattern: In general there is a strong seasonal pattern for deaths in New Zealand. Deaths are lowest in the summer (Q1) and highest in the winter (Q3). This sis due to the colder weather when people spend less time outside, so transmission of flu, colds, etc. is more likely to occur.
Unusual points and explanations: Deaths during the second and third quarters of 2020 were unusually low because lockdowns and mask wearing etc. due to Covid meant that transmission of colds and flu were much less likely.

5 Seasonal pattern: There is no clear seasonal pattern, but cases do appear to be more prevalent during the colder months of the year.
Unusual points and explanations: Unusual points are difficult to spot because the seasonal pattern is erratic. However, there was a spike in March 2018. No particular reason was found for this.

Recomposition

1 Peaks in April 2018 and March 2021 (reasons given in question **3** above).
Low point in April 2021.

2 There is a spike in June 2016 and another in March 2020 (reasons given in question **2** above).

B Forecast reliability (pp. 58–62)

1 The seasonal pattern is **consistent**/~~inconsistent.~~
This suggests the forecasts are likely to be **reliable**/~~unreliable~~.
The historical predictions **do**/~~do not~~ match up. This suggests the forecasts are likely to be **reliable**/~~unreliable.~~

ISBN: 9780170472975

Time	Total all cattle	
2021M01	255498	✓
2021M02	262985	✓
2021M03	335427	✓
2021M04	291931	✓
2021M05	346708	✓
2021M06	277093	✓
2021M07	457222	✓
2021M08	1113198	✓
2021M09	631445	✓
2021M10	284143	✓
2021M11	241782	✓
2021M12	232875	✓

The robustness check suggests the forecasts are \ likely to be **reliable**/~~unreliable.~~
Overall, these forecasts are likely to **reliable**/ ~~unreliable~~

2 The seasonal pattern is ~~consistent~~/**inconsistent**. This suggests the forecasts are likely to be ~~reliable~~/ **unreliable**.
The historical predictions ~~do~~/**do not** match up. This suggests the forecasts are likely to be ~~reliable~~/ **unreliable**.

Time	Total all pigs	
2021M01	47394	✗
2021M02	47904	✓
2021M03	57685	✓
2021M04	52151	✓
2021M05	52835	✓
2021M06	55518	✓
2021M07	53778	✓
2021M08	52994	✓
2021M09	51261	✓
2021M10	49870	✓
2021M11	56538	✓
2021M12	55600	✓

The robustness check suggests the forecasts are likely to be **reliable**/~~unreliable~~ **(apart from the January prediction)**.
Overall, these forecasts are likely to ~~reliable~~/ **unreliable (especially in the short term)**.

C Comparing variables (pp. 63–64)

1 There are a significantly more births in New Zealand than deaths. This would suggest that the population is growing.
Comparison suggests investigation of the age composition of the New Zealand population, and how it is changing.

2 There are far more sheep being slaughtered in New Zealand than cattle, and the peaks in numbers slaughtered are at different times of the year: sheep in midsummer and cattle in about July.
Sheep are much smaller than cattle, so it would be interesting to compare the total masses of sheep and cattle slaughtered.

Writing about time series data (pp. 72–73)

1 The trend shows that the number of deaths in New Zealand is increasing. However, in 2020 there is a decrease in the trend line. This **is likely to have been** due to the reduction in the number of influenza cases due to the Covid restrictions.

2 We can see from the graph that the imports of sugar have been decreasing and **are likely to** continue to decrease.

3 The seasonal graph shows **a similar** pattern each year.

4 The 95% confidence limits for the forecasts for the quarterly number of deaths in New Zealand in Q1 of 2022 are 7497 and 8831. This means that the actual number of deaths **is very likely to** lie between these numbers.

5 During the summer months in New Zealand there are fewer deaths because people **are less likely to** contract life-threatening illnesses.

6 There are several significant large residuals, which **suggests** that if this model is used to make predictions, they **may** not be accurate.

7 The model fits well, so forecasts for the next two years **are likely to be** reliable. They should give us **an approximate** amount of milk powder that will be exported from New Zealand.

8 The robustness check **suggests** that the predictions **may not be** entirely accurate.

9 The model is robust, **suggesting** that any predictions will **probably** be reliable.

10 The value of the residual is **exactly** the actual value minus the model value.

11 Forecasts beyond two cycles from the final piece of data **are less likely to be** reliable.

Pick the errors (p. 74)

1 a Average seasonal effects should be expressed as **either above or below** the trend. In this case, '144 010 tonnes of apples **above the trend**'.

b This has a **double negative**, so remove the negative sign. Should be '**is 84 477** tonnes of apples below the trend'.

2 Discrete data should be **rounded**. It is not possible to have 0.9 deaths. In this case, '**is about 8300**'.

3 Just because one prediction doesn't fall within the confidence interval doesn't mean short-term estimates won't be accurate.

4 The confidence intervals become larger to allow for greater variation in the future. We are still 95% confident the actual value will lie within the interval.

5 Not possible to have a negative number of meningococcal cases. In this case, 'will be **between 0 and 9**'.

6 No units. Should be 'of 2562.5 **tonnes** per year'.

7 No indication of the period (quarterly or monthly) used in the data. In this case, 'from 7620 **per**

ISBN: 9780170472975

quarter at the start of 2014 to 8970 per quarter in late 2021'. Alternatively, 'in the trend for the number of deaths per quarter in New Zealand'.

Practice tasks (pp. 81–92)

Practice task one (pp. 81–82)

1 Numbers of ice creams sold will not allow the canteen to know their profit: This will allow the canteen to know how many ice creams they are going to sell in the future.
2 The trend does not show the seasonal pattern: There is a seasonal pattern in which more are sold in summer and fewer in winter.
3 The trend shows an overall decrease, not an increase.
4 Data is per quarter, not per month.
5 The seasonal pattern is similar each year, it is not the same.
6 The third quarter is the lowest with about 669 below average, not -669 below. Double negative makes it a positive.
7 The prediction for the first quarter of 2022 is 1511; 1240 is the minimum of the confidence interval.

Practice task two (pp. 83–86)

Research and variable

The cost of living in New Zealand is the highest it's been since Statistics New Zealand began recording data in 2008. https://www.stats.govt.nz/news/increase-in-cost-of-living-reaches-new-high. While rent and petrol prices are increasing, one of the largest expenses to households in food. https://www.nzherald.co.nz/business/new-data-grocery-prices-push-food-bills-higher-in-april/LUSJKUN5E6Y5656RTC5UNGQXQQ/#:~:text=Food%20prices%206.4%20per%20cent%20higher%20than%20April%202021&text=Overall%20grocery%20food%20prices%20increased,prices%20increased%202.8%20per%20cent.
The variable is the amount spent on groceries in New Zealand in millions of dollars.

Purpose

I am going to investigate the amount of money spent on groceries per quarter in New Zealand. I am going to investigate this data because I would like to know if there has been an overall change in spending since the start of 2013, and whether there is a seasonal pattern. I will also find predictions for 2022, because these would be of use to grocery wholesalers and retailers for planning stock levels. Predictions based on this data might be useful for government, consumer organisations, charities that supply food parcels to needy families and the general public.

Trend

Between the start of 2013 and the end of 2021, there has been an overall increase in the amount spent on groceries in New Zealand of about $1 560 000 000, from $4 330 000 000 in 2013 to $5 890 000 000 in 2021. This is about a 36% increase.

The steepest increase in the amount spent occurred towards the end of 2019. After that it plateaued in 2020, probably because during lockdowns and periods with Covid restrictions. People tended to avoide shopping for groceries where possible, used stored supplies, and possibly ate less. In addition, restaurants were closed, or open with restrictions so they would have been buying less. This was followed by an increase throughout 2021.

Over the nine years, the average amount of quarterly spending increased by $1 560 000 000. The average increase in the amount of quarterly spending was $173 000 000 per year.

Seasonality

The amount spent during the first quarter of the year is close to the average, $82 000 000 above the trend. In the second quarter the amount spent is just under $156 000 000 below the average. In the third quarter the amount spent was at its lowest at about $168 000 000 below the average. The amount spent reaches its peak in the fourth quarter, when it is just under $229 000 000 above the average. This is probably partly because all the pre-Christmas festivities, end of year functions, Christmas itself and New Year fall into this quarter.

Forecast

The forecast is that the amount spent on groceries in New Zealand during q1 of 2022 will be about $6 010 000 000. We can be 95% confident that the actual amount will lie between $5 754 000 000 and $6 271 000 000. The forecast should be very reliable because the majority of the model is a fairly good fit for the data. The last couple of years the model doesn't fit quite as well however, this is likely due to covid.

Conclusion

The total amount spent on groceries each quarter in New Zealand has increased steadily from the start of 2013 until the end of 2021. The overall increase during the nine years was about 36 %. The largest amounts are spent during the warmest quarters, particularly in quarter four. The model was a fairly good fit for the data, so the predictions made should be very reliable. It would be interesting to investigate different groups of groceries, such as fresh fruit and vegetables, canned goods, dairy products, etc to see if these follow similar spending patterns.

Practice task three (pp. 87–92)

Beer

Research and choice of variable

With beer varieties being introduced to the New Zealand market regularly it won't be a surprise if there is an increase in the volume of beer available to be

ISBN: 9780170472975

consumed in New Zealand. It isn't necessarily all bad news for addiction agencies, as while the craft beer market is expanding so is the low-strength beer market. https://www.actionpoint.org.nz
The variable I have chosen is the total volume of beer available for consumption in New Zealand

Purpose
I am going to investigate the volume of beer available for consumption in New Zealand. I am going to investigate this data because I would like to know if there has been an overall change in consumption since 2012, and whether there is a seasonal pattern. I will also find predictions for 2022, because these would be of use to liquor wholesalers and retailers for planning stock levels, and organisations dealing with problems with alcohol addiction.

Trend
Between the start of 2012 and the end of 2021, there has been an overall increase in the volume of beer available for consumption about 0.26 million litres per quarter, from 3 million litres per quarter in 2012 to 3.26 million litres per quarter in 2021. This is about an 8% increase.

The increase has been steady throughout the ten years with little fluctuation.

Over the ten years, the average increase in the volume of beer available to be consumed is 260,000 litres per year. This steady increase may be a result of the increasing availability of craft and low alcohol beers in New Zealand.

Seasonality
During the first quarter of the year the volume of beer available for consumption is about 162,000 litres below the average. During the second quarter the volume available is at its lowest at about 402,000 litres below the average. This increases slightly to 286,000 below the average in quarter three. This is probably because a cold beer is less likely to be the drink of choice during the winter months. Availability is at its peak of about 879,000 litres above the average during the last quarter of the year, probably because all the pre-Christmas festivities, Christmas itself and New Year fall into this quarter.

Forecast
The forecast for quarter one of 2022 is that the volume of beer available to be consumed in New Zealand will be about 3.09 million litres. We can be 95% confident that this value will lie between 2.7795 and 3.4139 million litres. Because the model is a reasonably good fit for the data, we can be quite confident in the accuracy of this forecast.

Conclusion
Between the start of 2012 and the end of 2021 there has been about an 8% increase in the volume of beer available to be consumed in New Zealand. The seasonal pattern is consistent, with the largest volume of beer available in the fourth quarter, the lowest during the winter months.

Forecasts can be made with confidence because the model matched the data closely. This information would be useful for liquor retailers and wholesalers to plan how much stock they should order and hold, although there would always be a big demand in quarters one and four. The overall increase in the volume of alcohol available in beer would probably be of interest to organisations dealing with problems with alcohol addiction.

Optional extras:
1 In depth research and evidence of contextual knowledge.
2 Research to find reasons for unusual points.
3 More discussion about the accuracy of the forecast. Robustness check.
4 Combine the alcohol series to produce, for instance, a series showing the percentage of alcohol intake that comes from beer.
5 Compare information from the three sets of data to make comparisons between the alcohol types.

Spirits
Research and choice of variable
Spirits have become increasingly popular with younger people with the introduction of RTD's. While the government announced plans to reduce the maximum percentage of alcohol allowed in RTD's, this never came to fruition. While pure spirits are consumed more by older age groups, RTD's are increasingly preferred by younger people. https://www.actionpoint.org.nz
The variable I have chosen is the total volume of spirits available for consumption in New Zealand

Purpose
I am going to investigate the volume of spirits available for consumption in New Zealand. I am going to investigate this data because I would like to know if there has been an overall change in consumption since 2012, and whether there is a seasonal pattern. I will also find predictions for 2022, because these would be of use to liquor wholesalers and retailers for planning stock levels, and organisations dealing with problems with alcohol addiction.

Trend
Between the start of 2012 and the end of 2021, there has been an overall increase in the volume of spirits available for consumption about 0.6 million litres per quarter, from 2.53 million litres per quarter in 2012 to 3.13 million litres per quarter in 2021. This is about a 19% increase.

From 2012 until 2015 there was a decrease in the volume of spirits available for consumption, from 2015

ISBN: 9780170472975

there was a steady increase other than a small dip in 2019. Throughout 2020 and 2021 there has been increasing amounts of spirits available for consumption in New Zealand.

Over the ten years, the average increase in the volume of spirits available to be consumed is 600,000 litres per year.

Seasonality

During the first quarter of the year the volume of spirits available for consumption is at its lowest at around 358,000 litres below the average. During the second quarter the volume available increases to about 230,000 litres below the average. This increases in the third quarter to 105,000 above the average. Availability is at its peak of about 533,000 litres above the average during the last quarter of the year, probably because all the pre-Christmas festivities, Christmas itself and New Year fall into this quarter.

Forecast

The forecast for quarter one of 2022 is that the volume of spirits available to be consumed in New Zealand will be about 2.885 million litres. We can be 95% confident that this value will lie between 2.3915 and 3.3613 million litres. Because the model is not always a very good fit for the data, we cannot have great confidence in the accuracy of this forecast.

Conclusion

Between the start of 2012 and the end of 2021 there has been about a 19% increase in the volume of spirits available to be consumed in New Zealand. The seasonal pattern is consistent, with the largest volume of spirits available in the fourth quarter, the lowest during the first quarter.

Forecasts could not be made with great confidence because there was quite a lot of unaccounted for variability in the data, so the model did not always match the data closely. This must make it quite difficult for liquor retailers and wholesalers to plan how much stock they should order and hold, particularly because many spirits are imported. The overall increase in the volume of alcohol consumed in spirits would probably be of interest to organisations dealing with problems with alcohol addiction.

Optional extras:

1. In depth research and evidence of contextual knowledge.
2. Research to find reasons for unusual points.
3. More discussion about the accuracy of the forecast. Robustness check.
4. Combine the alcohol series to produce, for instance, a series showing the percentage of alcohol intake that comes from spirits.
5. Compare information from the three sets of data to make comparisons between the alcohol types.

Wine

Research and choice of variable

Wine consumption in New Zealand has increased since it was available for sale in supermarkets in 1989. Wine is a major export for the country and the second most popular form of alcohol. This may be because it partners well with food, and during this period the range and quality of New Zealand wines have both increased substantially. White wine is almost twice as popular than red. https://www.actionpoint.org.nz The variable I have chosen is the total volume of wine available for consumption in New Zealand.

Purpose

I am going to investigate the volume of wine available for consumption in New Zealand. I am going to investigate this data because I would like to know if there has been an overall change in consumption since 2012, and whether there is a seasonal pattern. I will also find predictions for 2022, because these would be of use to liquor wholesalers and retailers for planning stock levels, and organisations dealing with problems with alcohol addiction.

Trend

Between the start of 2012 and the end of 2021, there has been an overall increase in the volume of wine available for consumption about 0.23 million litres per quarter, from 2.68 million litres per quarter in 2012 to 2.91 million litres per quarter in 2021. This is about an 8% increase.

The increase has been steady throughout the ten years with little fluctuation.

Over the ten years, the average increase in the volume of wine available to be consumed is 230,000 litres per year.

Seasonality

During the first quarter of the year the volume of wine available for consumption is at its lowest at around 376,000 litres below the average. During the second quarter the amount available increases to about 136,000 litres below the average. This increases in the third quarter to 82,000 below the average. Availability is at its peak of about 606,000 litres above the average during the last quarter of the year, probably because all the pre-Christmas festivities, Christmas itself and New Year fall into this quarter.

Forecast

The forecast for quarter one of 2022 is that the volume of spirits available to be consumed in New Zealand will be about 2.3428 million litres. We can be 95% confident that this value will lie between 2.0723 and 2.6004 million litres. Because the model is a reasonably good fit for the data, we can be quite confident in the accuracy of this forecast.

Conclusion

Between the start of 2012 and the end of 2021 there has been about a 8% increase in the volume of wine available to be consumed in New Zealand. The seasonal pattern is consistent, with the largest volume of wine available in the fourth quarter, the lowest during the first quarter.

Forecasts can be made with confidence because the model matched the data closely. This information would be useful for liquor retailers and wholesalers to plan how much stock they should order and hold, although there would always be a big demand in quarters one and four. The overall increase in the volume of alcohol available in beer would probably be of interest to organisations dealing with problems with alcohol addiction.

Optional extras:

1. In depth research and evidence of contextual knowledge.
2. Research to find reasons for unusual points.
3. More discussion about the accuracy of the forecast. Robustness check.
4. Combine the alcohol series to produce, for instance, a series showing the percentage of alcohol intake that comes from wine.
5. Compare information from the three sets of data to make comparisons between the alcohol types.

ISBN: 9780170472975